THE STORY OF EXPLORATION

EXPLORING
DESERTS

ABDO
Publishing Company

THE STORY OF EXPLORATION

EXPLORING DESERTS

BY KAREN SIRVAITIS

CONTENT CONSULTANT
NICHOLAS LANCASTER, PHD
RESEARCH PROFESSOR
DESERT RESEARCH INSTITUTE

CREDITS

Published by ABDO Publishing Company, PO Box 398166, Minneapolis, MN 55439. Copyright © 2014 by Abdo Consulting Group, Inc. International copyrights reserved in all countries. No part of this book may be reproduced in any form without written permission from the publisher. The Essential Library™ is a trademark and logo of ABDO Publishing Company.

Printed in the United States of America,
North Mankato, Minnesota
102013
012014

 THIS BOOK CONTAINS AT LEAST 10% RECYCLED MATERIALS.

Editor: Rebecca Felix
Series Designer: Emily Love

Photo credits: iStockphoto/Thinkstock, cover, 1, 14, 22, 26, 38 (bottom left, bottom right), 42 (left, right), 46–47, 62, 74–75, 98–99, 113, 123, 128–129, 133 (bottom left, bottom right); Konrad Wothe/Minden Pictures/Getty Images, 6–7; Dorling Kindersley RF/Thinkstock, 9, 20–21, 132; Classic Image/Alamy, 16–17; Shutterstock Images, 24; ilbusca/iStockphoto, 29; Hulton Archive/iStockphoto, 30–31; Michael Nicholson/Corbis, 32–33; akg-images/Newscom, 37; Science & Society Picture Library/SSPL/Getty Images, 38 (top left); Hemera/Thinkstock, 38 (top right); Photos.com/Getty Images/Thinkstock, 41, 133 (top left); Public Domain, 44; Fine Art Photographic Library/Corbis, 48–49; Mary Evans Picture Library/Everett Collection, 51, 59; Design Pics/Newscom, 52–53; Timothy H. O'Sullivan/Library of Congress, 56–57; Everett Collection, 60–61; STR/Reuters/Newscom, 64–65; Martin Valent/Shutterstock Images, 67; akg-images/Werner Forman/Newscom, 69; Red Line Editorial, 70–71, 90–91; AP Images, 77, 133 (top right); Mary Evans/Grenville Collins Postcard Collection/Everett Collection, 78–79; Jesse Allen and Robert Simmon/NASA/GSFC/METI/ERSDAC/JAROS and U.S./Japan, ASTER Science Team, 82; Yuma Daily Sun, Paul M. Perez/AP Images, 85; Keystone/Getty Images, 88; Keystone-France/Gamma-Keystone via Getty Images, 93; 80eight Photography & Design/Alamy, 97; Carlos Barria/Reuters/Newscom, 102–103; Augustane College/AP Images, 108; Yingling/MCT/Newscom, 111; George Frey/EPA/Newscom, 114–115; Ernersto Benavides/AFP/Getty Images/Newscom, 118–119; University of Arizona, Kevin Fitzsimmons/AP Images, 124

Library of Congress Control Number: 2013946598
Cataloging-in-Publication Data

Sirvaitis, Karen.
 Exploring deserts / Karen Sirvaitis.
  p. cm. -- (The story of exploration)
Includes bibliographical references and index.
ISBN 978-1-62403-250-9
1. Deserts--Juvenile literature. 2. Desert ecology--Juvenile literature. 3. Deserts--Discovery and exploration--Juvenile literature. I. Title.
551.41--dc23

2013946598

CONTENTS

Local people call Mount Idinen
the Palace of the Demons
because they believe spirits
gather there to pray and use
the desert mountain to store
their treasures.

THE ALLURE OF THE DESERT

CHAPTER 1

Near Mount Idinen, a colorful desert mountain also known as the Palace of the Demons and sacred to locals in Libya, North Africa, a young, ambitious scientist lay, waiting to die. Against all warnings, he had left his caravan to explore the sacred mountain for ancient stone carvings. When members of the scientist's expedition discovered his absence, they formed a search party. They lit bonfires, hoping to direct him toward camp. Out of water and dying of thirst, the scientist slit his arm and drank his own blood, an act that may have saved his life. Delirious,

7

and with a dry throat swollen from dehydration, the scientist could not even swallow when his rescuers arrived with water.

The young scientist was German explorer Heinrich Barth. It was August 1850, the hottest time of year in the Sahara desert, where the mountain range containing the Palace of the Demons is located. Barth was missing for more than 24 hours. Surviving the climate for this long was a feat itself. According to local guides, most people can survive only 12 hours without water in such hot and dry conditions. But Barth went on to study the region and share his knowledge with other Europeans. Although Barth survived, throughout history, many people curious and daring enough to explore the deserts did not live to tell about it, including two of Barth's traveling companions in later expeditions.

DEFINING DESERTS

Desert covers approximately one-third of Earth's land surface.[1] Each of the world's seven continents contains deserts, and they even exist on the planet Mars. Some

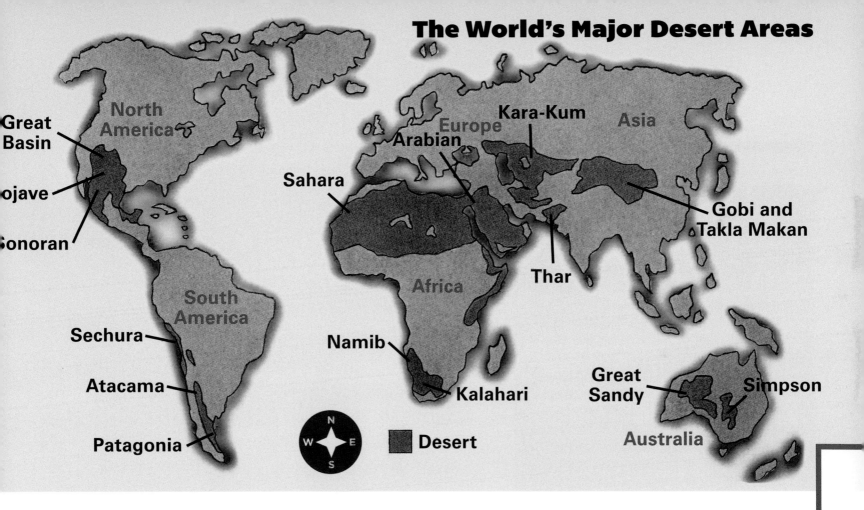

The World's Major Desert Areas

Great Basin

North America

Mojave

Sonoran

Sechura

South America

Atacama

Patagonia

Sahara

Europe

Arabian

Kara-Kum

Asia

Gobi and Takla Makan

Thar

Africa

Namib

Kalahari

Great Sandy

Simpson

Australia

N W E S

■ **Desert**

people think of a desert as barren and useless land. Others
picture a sea of soft, swirling sand. Still others think of the
plants and wildlife—prickly saguaro cacti or the deadly

DESERT EXTREMES

The largest and coldest desert in the world is the continent of Antarctica, which spans 5.5 million square miles (14.2 million sq km) across the South Pole.[3] On July 21, 1983, at the Vostok Station in central Antarctica, the temperature reached a brutally frigid minus 128.6 degrees Fahrenheit (−89.2°C), the coldest temperature ever recorded on Earth.[4]

The largest hot desert is the Sahara in North Africa. On September 13, 1922, the temperature in the Libyan Sahara reached a sizzling 136 degrees Fahrenheit (58°C), the hottest temperature ever recorded on Earth.[5] The Sahara spans 3.32 million square miles (8.6 million sq km).[6] This is nearly the size of the continental United States!

The world's driest desert is the Atacama in South America. The average rainfall is 0.004 inches (0.01 cm) per year, or 4 inches (10 cm) every 1,000 years.[7] In some areas of this coastal desert, rain has not fallen since humankind started keeping record.[8]

bite of a rattlesnake or scorpion. Deserts of the world vary greatly. They can consist of sand, salt flats, vegetation, rocks, plateaus, mountains, and even ice. Deserts can be hot or cold. Average desert temperatures range from zero to 120 degrees Fahrenheit (-18 to 49°C), depending on the location, season, and time of day.[2] Deserts can be void of water for hundreds of miles, contain lagoons or lakes, or butt up against an ocean. Some deserts are without rainfall for long periods of time, while others experience flash floods. To be called a desert, the only requirement is that the area receives on average less than ten inches (25 cm) per year in rainfall.[9]

DESERT EXPLORATION

Reasons for desert exploration have changed during the course of history. Thousands of years ago, ancient desert dwellers throughout the world learned about the desert in order to survive in it. In some places, such as the Sahara, climates changed from wet to dry, and people had to adapt to the new conditions. The Bedouin, a nomadic group of people from the Middle East and North Africa, are one example. The Bedouin learned to move frequently with their animal herds in order to find food and water.

DESERT RAINS

Rainfall is controlled by atmospheric conditions, including wind patterns and cloud formation, as well as geography. Subtropical deserts such as the Sahara are located north or south of the equator, along the Tropic of Capricorn and the Tropic of Cancer. Areas along the equator experience Earth's highest temperatures. Hot, moist air rises above the equator and cools as it reaches the upper atmosphere, releasing heavy tropical rains. This creates cool, dry air that descends and moves away from the equator. This air warms up again as it moves toward the tropics and obstructs clouds from forming. The result is the land below receives very little rainfall. Coastal deserts, such as the Atacama in Chile, are often foggy but dry. These conditions are the result of thermal inversion: the air at sea level is cold, chilled by the ocean currents, while the air above it is warm. Air masses reach the shore full of moisture, in the form of fog. Thermal inversion naturally blocks the creation of rain.

Interest in desert exploration grew over the centuries, especially for Europeans and Americans. Some explorers ventured into the desert because they were intrigued by cultures and lands different from their own.

Some people explored deserts for religious purposes, bent on spreading their beliefs. Spies, politicians, and military leaders who explored the deserts of the world often did so in hopes of conquering the region and its people or to control strategic desert resources, such as oil. Other early explorers were scientists who sought to find unfamiliar plants, animals, landscapes, or ancient treasures. Various artists throughout the centuries captured the natural beauty of deserts in works of art. Many recent exploratory efforts focus on desert farming and studying and protecting the desert environment.

Desert explorers have traveled thousands of miles through unfamiliar land with extreme climates to reach new terrain. These explorers faced many obstacles and uncertainties in their quests, including disorientation, fever, fatigue, dust storms, flash floods, unfamiliar cultures and languages, and lack of water, food, and shelter. Many desert explorers risked their lives for the sake of knowledge and duty. Some did so for fame. Being the first known European to enter a desert in Africa or Asia was exhilarating. Most expeditions were funded by governments or geographic societies interested in learning more about a particular area.

Desert explorers often became passionate about and felt deep affection for the dry terrains they studied. Historian Bill Kennedy Shaw, who spent time in the Sahara during the first part of the 1900s, summed up his feelings about the desert:

> *Although in it one saw Nature at her hardest, yet it was a*

DUST STORMS IN THE SAHARA

Harmattans are strong trade winds that produce dust storms. These winds are most common and account for the majority of dust storms in the southern Sahara and West Africa but are less dramatic than another type of wind. Haboob is a powerful wind that blows across a dry region, creating intense sand or dust storms. The word *haboob* comes from *habb*, the Arabic word for "wind." While haboobs can occur in any dry area, the name originated in the southern Sahara in Sudan, Africa, where haboobs are common and usually occur without warning. In Libya, the same type of dust storm is called the *ghibli*.

Haboobs can last from minutes to a few hours and can include thunder. During a haboob, winds can blow 60 miles per hour (97 kmh) or more, forming a wall of sand that can reach up to 10,000 feet (3,048 m) high, creating problems for pilots.[10]

country which many of us, I think, in time began to love. Its attraction for me was that it was so clean. . . . Also because it was quiet, at times so silent that you found yourself listening for something to hear. And it was beautiful too, not at midday when the hills look flat and lifeless, but in the early morning or late evening when they throw cool, dark shadows and the low sun makes you marvel at the splendid symmetry of the yellow dunes.[11]

Desert explorers today witness the same beauty— and face many of the same challenges—earlier explorers encountered. The desire to learn more about deserts continues inspiring exploration.

Features such as the massive, velvety sand dunes of the Sahara or the deep red and orange canyons and towering rock monuments of deserts worldwide have long inspired exploration.

Wells have been essential to desert survival since ancient times, as has the use of camels for travel and work.

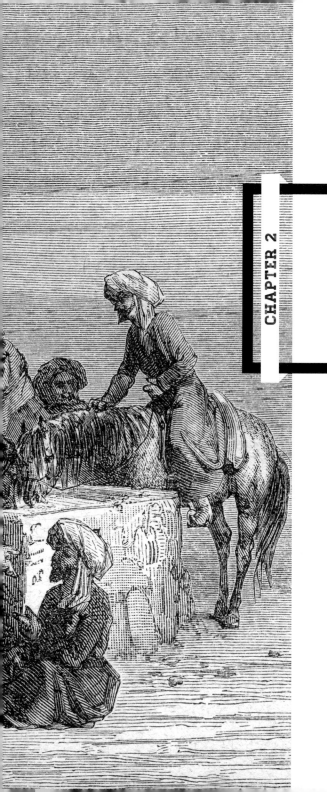

CHAPTER 2

DESERT SURVIVAL: WATER, SALT, AND CAMELS

Desert exploration began in prehistoric times as a necessity. To survive in the dry, harsh conditions, early desert dwellers had to learn some of the deserts' hidden secrets. They learned how to collect and store water, harvest salt from lakebeds, irrigate crops, find shelter to protect themselves from the sun and heat, and preserve food and the bodies of their dead. Surviving in the desert took skill, creativity, and the heart of an explorer. Today's desert dwellers and explorers still rely on many of these ancient methods of survival.

CREATING DESERT SHELTER: BEDOUIN BLACK TENT DWELLINGS

The Bedouin are a group of nomadic, Arabic-speaking animal herders who live in northern Africa and the Middle East. During the rainy season in the Middle East, the Bedouin move with their livestock to the desert. They have maintained this lifestyle for centuries using portable black tents for shelter.

Also called a house of hair, the tents get their names from their primary source of material: black goat hair. The Bedouin weave goat hair into long strips of cloth and sew them together to create a large rectangle approximately 100 to 130 feet (30 to 40 m) long. They erect it with ropes, creating a flat, wind-resistant roof. The side that does not face the wind remains open, except on the coldest nights. The black tent provides shade and protection from sandstorms.

DESERT WATER SOURCES

The driest place on Earth is the center of the Atacama, a cool desert that spans more than 600 miles (966 km) along the coast of northern Chile in South America.[1] Throughout most of the desert, rainfall is sparse or nonexistent. Yet, for hundreds of years, the Atacama and Aymara Indians have called this desert home.

In the best of conditions, humans can survive without water for only one week. Just 12 summer hours in a dry desert without water can be deadly. How—and where—did ancient desert dwellers find water to survive?

In deserts around the world, the most common sources of water are rivers and streams, groundwater, and the occasional rainfall. Early desert dwellers were able to find water from these sources to drink, irrigate crops, bathe in, and store for later use.

Rivers, streams, and rainfall provided visible water sources in ancient times. But early desert dwellers needed to explore for groundwater, which is usually hidden below the surface of the earth. Groundwater collects in small spaces within layers of permeable rock underground called aquifers. Aquifers are filled by rainwater that seeps into the earth's surface. The Aborigines, indigenous inhabitants of Australia, discovered groundwater sources by studying nature. They followed dingoes, native Australian dogs, to water holes where groundwater seeped to the surface. On dry surfaces, an ant colony was a sign groundwater lay beneath the surface, letting the Aborigines know where to dig. Many early desert dwellers also dug shallow wells

spring

aquifer

Water from an underground
artesian aquifer flows below
the surface of the earth,
sometimes breaking the
surface as a desert spring.

so groundwater could bubble up to the surface. As cultures developed more sophisticated tools, people dug deeper wells and lined them with bricks to prevent the water from seeping back into the ground.

CONSTRUCTING WATER ACCESS

Another method for collecting groundwater is a *qanat*, a series of sloping tunnels built underground to trap water from mountain streams. Persians in what is now Iran began building qanats approximately 3,000 years ago. Some ancient qanats are still used in

ARTESIAN WATER IN THE AUSTRALIAN DESERT

The land mass of the continent Australia is classified as 20 percent desert.[2] Stored beneath much of this desert is one of the world's largest sources of artesian water. Called the Great Artesian Basin, the huge underground water basin covers approximately 670,000 square miles (1.7 million sq km), or one-fifth of the continent of Australia.[3] The basin exists mainly below the Simpson Desert in central Australia. It has 18,000 boreholes, or small holes drilled into the surface of the earth to obtain water held in the basin. Through these boreholes, the basin releases approximately 350 million gallons (1.3 billion L) of artesian water per day.[4] However, evaporation and seepage cause much of this water to be lost. Australians distribute water that is not lost from the basin for watering animals or agriculture.

Iran and Afghanistan today. The city of Yazd, Iran, boasts the largest network of qanats in the world.

Beginning approximately 1,500 years ago in the Thar Desert of India, it was common for royal families to build step wells to access water. A step well featured steps made of stone that often descended several tens of feet below Earth's surface. Each step well led to a reservoir of groundwater. Step wells also stored water from seasonal monsoons for use throughout the year. Other ancient desert communities, such as the Hohokam Indians in what is now central and southern Arizona, built elaborate canals and irrigation systems to harness water sources.

Today, desert farmers irrigate crops using center pivots, which are sprinkler towers on wheels that move in a circle. Center pivots tap into fossil groundwater that was created eons ago and has remained trapped deep underground, sealed in aquifers.

The Chand Baori lies at the edge of the Thar Desert in India and is one of the country's oldest and deepest step wells.

The Nile River is a bustling and vital center of life for desert dwellers, providing water, power, travel, and food resources.

Rivers are also used for desert irrigation. In the United States, the Colorado River supports life throughout the three major deserts it crosses: the Great Basin, the Mojave, and the Sonoran. The fertile shores of the Tigris and Euphrates Rivers in present-day Iraq supported the development of the Sumerians, one of the world's earliest civilizations. In Africa, the Nile River is a valuable source of water. It is the longest river in the world at 4,132 miles (6,650 km).[5] The northern stretch of the river runs through the eastern Sahara, providing the most reliable source of water for all aspects of daily life in the region, including irrigation, drinking, and bathing. Completed in 1970, the Aswan High Dam was built near the Egyptian-Sudanese border to harness Nile water for hydroelectric power. It corrals the river water into Lake Nasser, which can store a supply of water during river droughts.

Water is the most important element required for surviving in the desert. But early desert cultures also pursued another element that was less obvious but still key to human survival: salt.

WHITE GOLD

Salt is a mineral that is essential for life. It is needed in order for the body to maintain fluid in blood cells, transmit information in nerves and muscles, and absorb nutrients from the stomach. A person needs to consume an estimated 1 to 16 pounds (0.5 to 7 kg) of salt each year to maintain

Flat, dry areas where lakes or rivers have dried up and left salt behind, such as the Badwater Basin in Death Valley, California, are known as salt flats.

proper health.[6] One way the body loses salt is through sweating. In the dry desert, people lose salt quickly from sweating and must replace the salt they lose. Without salt, muscle cramping, headaches, nausea, and death are possible.

Early desert dwellers in Egypt also realized salt could be used as a preservative. They noticed the bodies of their deceased who were buried at the edge of the dry and salty Sahara did not decay. Salt was then used as a preservative, applied to fish and meat to dry them out and keep them edible for longer. As early as the 500s CE, the Chinese began using salt to ferment vegetables. This practice involved curing vegetables in a salty solution for a long period of time and then storing them for consumption at a later date, when fresh crops were not available.

Because of its necessity to life and food preservation, salt is a valuable trade commodity. Some have even called it "white gold."[7] Dry lakebeds, such as the Great Salt Lake Desert in present-day Utah, are a primary source of salt. Early desert dwellers harvested salt by scraping it from dry lakes and riverbeds as early as 6000 BCE. By the Middle Ages (600–1400s CE), salt was a widely traded commodity around the world. In the Sahara, caravans of camels numbering into the tens of thousands trekked hundreds of miles across the desert to deliver salt from salt mining towns such as Taghaza in present-day Mali to Timbuktu, a trading post just north of the Niger River in Mali.

CAMEL TRAVEL

As early as 3000 BCE, desert dwellers in the Middle East domesticated the wild dromedary camel, using it for transportation and to carry goods and supplies across the deserts. Camels are ideal for desert exploration because they can go without water for long periods of time. Depending on the weather, how much moisture is in the vegetation they eat, and how heavy a load they are carrying, camels can survive anywhere from four days to ten months without drinking water. Nomadic desert tribes also consumed the animal's milk and meat, wove the

TAGHAZA: CITY OF SALT

From the 1200s through the 1500s, Taghaza in northern Mali in West Africa, was an important mining town. The city was located in the Sahara on a salt pan, or dry lake, and supplied salt rock to Mali's flourishing salt trade. Slaves worked Taghaza's salt pan in the desert heat and sun and then retired to houses and mosques made of blocks of salt with camel skins as rooftops. While the town produced wealth for traders, its resources did not sustain life for the slaves. Slaves were entirely dependent on caravans to bring them food and water, as the soil was too salty to support any vegetation and the groundwater too briny to drink.

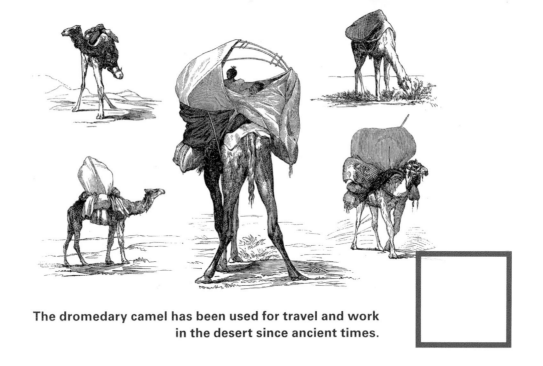

The dromedary camel has been used for travel and work in the desert since ancient times.

hair into fabric, and burned the dung as a source of fuel—
and still do today.

Camels have almost always been the transportation of
choice in most hot deserts. By the 1800s, Europeans took
an interest in the desert landscape. Most of them relied on
camel caravans to transport the people and supplies needed
for their usually lengthy and event-filled expeditions.

Explorers traversed the arid Australian outback in the 1800s in order to make new discoveries and map the terrain.

CHAPTER 3

SLAVERY AND SCIENCE

Over the centuries, the reasons for desert exploration expanded beyond survival and trade. The desire to expand scientific knowledge, map uncharted lands, and spread religious beliefs drew explorers to arid landscapes around the world. By the mid-1800s, people unaccustomed to desert living risked their lives not only to traverse deserts for science and adventure but also to try to end a practice that had been in place for centuries.

Slaves being transported
through the African desert

SLAVERY

Slavery was legal during ancient times throughout most of the world. By 1500 CE, the transatlantic slave trade took root. Africans were captured and brought to the Atlantic Coast and sold to European slave traders. The Europeans took the captives by ship across the Atlantic Ocean to the New World, where they were sold to people who needed laborers in the Caribbean and in the Americas. By the 1800s, Christian missionaries from Europe and the United States were determined to eliminate slavery. Although the United States no longer imported slaves by the early 1800s, slavery was still common in parts of the country, as well as in parts of Africa and the Middle East.

One missionary who sought to end slavery across the globe was James Richardson, a British minister. Richardson began his efforts in Islamic Africa, where he planned to spread Christianity and end the slave trade. After spending some time in North Africa gathering information about the slave trade, Richardson determined the only way to end slavery was to open trade between Africa and Europe. His hope was that African leaders who grew rich selling slaves could profit in other ways, by trading goods such as salt and dates with the large European market. In exchange, the tribal leaders would sign agreements giving up the practice of raiding villages and capturing people to sell overseas or within Africa.

THE INHOSPITABLE SAHARA

Before trade between Africa and Europe could increase, trade routes had to be located and

ISLAMIC AFRICA

The religion of Islam is practiced by Muslims. It was founded in the 600s CE by the prophet Muhammad in Saudi Arabia. The religion spread quickly from the Middle East to Africa, partly because Arabs had been crossing the Sahara, the Red Sea, and the Indian Ocean for centuries to trade with Africans. They were accustomed to desert travel, and they were experienced sea traders. The Arabs were not hindered by the geographic barriers.

In Africa, Islam first took hold in Egypt and eventually spread westward across the Sahara into Tunisia, Algeria, and Morocco. Islam was not accepted easily by all North Africans until the 1100s CE, when Arab traders gained political power in North Africa. From that point on, Arabs became the dominant ethnic group and Islam the dominant religion in North Africa.

mapped. Ancient trade routes existed through the Sahara, but in the mid-1800s, Europeans knew very little about Africa. The Muslims of Islamic North Africa forbade or discouraged most Christians from entering their lands. Many parts of North Africa had never been seen by a European, and the maps that did exist were unreliable. Some were made up from literary descriptions of deserts in travel books, such as Ibn Battutah's *Rihlah*. The vast, formidable Sahara desert that spans North Africa was another major barrier, with its unbearably high temperatures, dust storms, swarms of flies, and impassable dunes. Over the years, hundreds of European explorers died of fever, dysentery, dehydration, or from violence while trying to pass through the Sahara.

By the end of 1849, Richardson had organized an expedition. It included two

IBN BATTUTAH

Ibn Battutah lived in the 1300s and is considered by some historians as one of the greatest medieval travelers. Battutah was born in Tangier, Morocco. He traveled more than 75,000 miles (120,700 km), mostly through lands in the Middle East, Africa, and Asia.[1] Battutah's journeys took him across many deserts. He published details about his travels in a book titled *Rihlah,* meaning "travels" in Arabic. It became a world-famous travel book.

German scientists, Heinrich Barth and Adolf Overweg.

The three Europeans and their African guides were headed into the harsh unknown of the Sahara with a long to-do list. Although they would keep the main goal of ending the slave trade in focus, the expedition had multiple additional purposes: to determine and map trade routes, negotiate trade agreements with African leaders that included the guaranteed safety of European traders, learn about the people and cultures, and study the plants, animals, and geography of the desert.

The explorers' supplies included everything from swords and tents to an assortment of medicines. The medicines would

DESERT SLAVE TRANSPORT

For many captured East African slaves, the road to captivity began with a 1,120-mile (1,800 km) trek across North Africa deserts on an ancient trade route called the Darb el Arba'in, which is Arabic for "the Forty Days' Road."[2] The route passes from Sudan to Egypt. At the height of the slave trade, it was used to transport caravans of as many as 2,000 camels and 1,000 slaves, as well as goods.[3] Surviving the route meant enduring the desert heat, flies, and meager rations of food and water. Camels, burdened with heavy loads, might last eight days without water, the length of time it takes to get from one water source to another on the trail. If a camel died for any reason, it was common practice for people on the trail to drink its blood and the water left in its stomach. The number of people and camels lost to dehydration and fatigue on the trail numbered in the thousands over the years. Their bones, preserved in the dry air and bleached white from the sun, still litter the trail.

James Richardson, Adolf Overweg, and Heinrich Barth

come in handy for fever and dysentery. Just as important, the explorers would need to give them as gifts to bandits and local leaders along their journey. They also hauled a disassembled boat, which they could reassemble in order to explore and survey Lake Chad in Africa. Barth and Overweg brought along a long list of scientific instruments

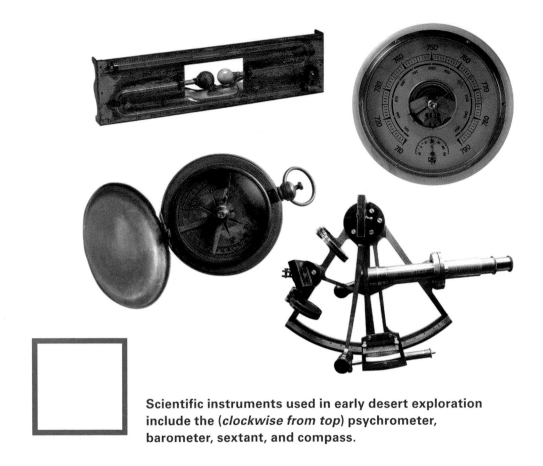

Scientific instruments used in early desert exploration include the (*clockwise from top*) psychrometer, barometer, sextant, and compass.

common at the time: compasses, telescopes, thermometers, sextants to measure latitude and longitude, a barometer for measuring atmospheric pressure, a psychrometer for measuring humidity, and chains for measuring distance.

Even before the group reached Africa, Barth and Overweg proved to be better traveling companions than Richardson, who tended to "dawdle."[4] They left Europe and sailed across the Mediterranean Sea to North Africa two weeks ahead of Richardson. This pattern continued throughout the two-year journey. The two scientists were anxious to get on with their explorations and were often two or more weeks ahead of the caravan. Barth's overwhelming urge to explore ahead of the caravan sometimes got him into trouble—as when he ventured to the Palace of the Demons.

Although well intentioned, Richardson's journey ended in disappointment, followed by his death toward the expedition's end from unknown causes. His exploits made little or no impact on slavery. Islamic traders had no intention of sharing their trade routes with European traders, and African leaders had no desire to give up the profitable slave trade. The minister did, however, leave behind useful notes about culture and geography of the desert.

Overweg also died toward the end of the expedition from a fever. He left no written accounts of the journey. Barth, however, went on to explore North and Central Africa over a five-year period, traversing 10,000 miles (16,093 km), mostly over desert.[5]

THE GREAT GAME

By the late 1800s, the world's political boundaries were changing rapidly. Russia and the United Kingdom held two of the largest empires in the world. The United Kingdom's imperial rule reached across most continents and included India. Russia's southern border was the Caspian Sea. Between the Caspian Sea and western China lies what is commonly referred to as central Asia. This area covers approximately 1.5 million square miles (3.8 million sq km), and approximately 60 percent of the region is desert.[6]

Beginning in the 1870s, central Asia became the location of what was known as the Great Game, during which the United Kingdom and Russia raced to conquer the area. National leaders, explorers, scientists, and spies

EXPLORER IN FOCUS
HEINRICH BARTH

Heinrich Barth spent the years between 1849 and 1854 traveling across Islamic Africa. Barth did not receive as much attention or credit as other explorers of his time did due to several reasons. One is because he told Christian Europeans who wanted to convert Islamic Africans to Christianity that he believed Islam was a great religion. Barth admired the African people and thought them beautiful. His ideas were in contrast to Europeans' generally held belief at the time that Africa was barbaric, giving Europeans reason to conquer its people and install new governments.

Barth wrote *Travels and Discoveries in North and Central Africa,* a five-volume book chronicling his experiences. Today, many consider Barth's book an invaluable resource on African history.

The landscape of the expansive Gobi Desert that Przhevalsky crossed during his central Asian expeditions varies from silky sand dunes to rocky canyons.

were involved in the Great Game, which included exploring central Asia to determine what resources existed within it. At the time, few Europeans had ever entered central Asia. Most of those who attempted to explore the area died trying. One Russian army officer, Nikolay Mikhaylovich

Przhevalsky, was one of several explorers during this time who led the way in mapping central Asia for these political interests.

EXPLORING ASIAN DESERTS

In 1870, Przhevalsky, a young Russian officer, naturalist, and cartographer, set out on his first expedition to explore and map uncharted lands in central Asia, including its deserts. Over the next 15 years, on four separate expeditions, Przhevalsky traveled by foot, camel, and horseback approximately 20,000 miles (32,187 km).[7] During these expeditions, he crossed Mongolia's Gobi Desert and the Takla Makan in China more than once.

Despite the intense desert heat, Przhevalsky and his group traveled by day rather than during the cooler night. This gave him the light he needed to create maps along the way. The surveying equipment Przhevalsky used to make his desert maps aroused suspicion among local populations. They had never seen a tripod or a compass, for instance. Przhevalsky took his measurements as

Nikolay Mikhaylovich Przhevalsky

discreetly as possible to avoid upsetting the locals over a miscommunication or misunderstanding about what the equipment did or was used for.

The explorers also encountered hungry wolves during their journeys. The wolves' main interest was the expedition's food supply. The animals dug up the group's caches and repeatedly stole food from their campsites.

In exploring central Asia, Przhevalsky's ultimate goal was to be the first European to reach Lhasa, the Forbidden City of Tibet. However, Tibetan troops heard rumors that Przhevalsky was in Tibet to kidnap revered Tibetan spiritual leader the Dalai Lama. The troops forced him to turn back. Przhevalsky never reached Lhasa. But the information he brought back to Russia about the people, land, animals, and plant life of central Asia made him a national hero. Przhevalsky returned to Russia with 16,000 plant and animal specimens, almost all of which

THE FORBIDDEN CITY OF LHASA

In the Tibetan language, Lhasa means "place of the Gods." Lhasa is the capital of Tibet, a region of China. At 11,975 feet (3,650 m) above sea level, it is one of the highest cities in the world.[8] The city is a sacred place to Tibetans, and foreigners were not allowed to enter it for many years. The intrigue of visiting a forbidden city and the political desire to conquer central Asia made Lhasa the goal of many Western explorers in the 1800s. Getting to Lhasa, however, was no small task. The trek included crossing thousands of miles of desert and confronting Tibetan troops who barred foreigners from entering the city. This type of confrontation occurred because the region was beginning to assert its independence from China. It officially declared its independence in 1912. Struggle for control remains today between the region and the Chinese government.

Europeans had never seen before.[9] Many of the specimens came from the desert, including the hide of an ancient breed of wild horse given to Przhevalsky by a local hunter. The expedition also encountered a herd of the wild horses in the Jungaar Desert in Mongolia. The sandy-colored horses were able to go days without water, having adapted to desert life.

Przhevalsky mapped a large section of central Asia during his expeditions, including the deserts. Russia was anxious to supply its central Asian spies with reliable information, making Przhevalsky's information and maps very valuable. Explorer Sven Hedin also led several expeditions through central Asian deserts, contributing to geologic findings and creating maps. Meanwhile, across the globe in the United States, deserts began inspiring travel and exploration for new purposes as well.

The wild horses Przhevalsky discovered in Mongolia were later named after him, today often recognized by the variant spelling Przewalski's horse. They are the last living subspecies of wild horse surviving in the 2000s.

A 1905 painting by Otto Pilny titled *In the Desert* depicts an exotic scene of a desert's landscape and people.

CHAPTER 4

ROMANTICIZING THE DESERT: TRAVEL AND ART

By the late 1800s and early 1900s, the focus of desert exploration began changing. People were looking at the desert not as a place to study or conquer but as a place of beauty and nostalgia. Photographers, writers, filmmakers, and other artists began depicting deserts in writing and works of art. Some of these artists expressed a romantic or idealized view of the desert, while others documented the people and places of the desert. The artists' works encouraged many people to visit deserts.

DEVELOPMENT OF DESERT TOURISM

Tourism has been around since before the Middle Ages. But in the mid-1800s, it was becoming common for middle-class people to become amateur explorers in their own right. People began traveling and paying to see some of the extraordinary sites they had read about in books or seen in pictures. British writer Lady Anne Blunt lived among the Bedouin to learn about their desert culture and shared her experience in her book *Bedouin Tribes of the Euphrates*. In the United States, writer Mark Twain helped to launch the "Tourist Age" by writing stories about his travels in the deserts of the Middle East, California, and Nevada.[1] In 1867, San Francisco, California, newspaper the *Daily Alta California* sent Twain to Europe and the deserts of North Africa and the Middle East. The paper's editor wanted him to write letters about his tourist experiences for the newspaper to publish. Twain had mixed reactions about the deserts he came across, but he fell in love when he first saw

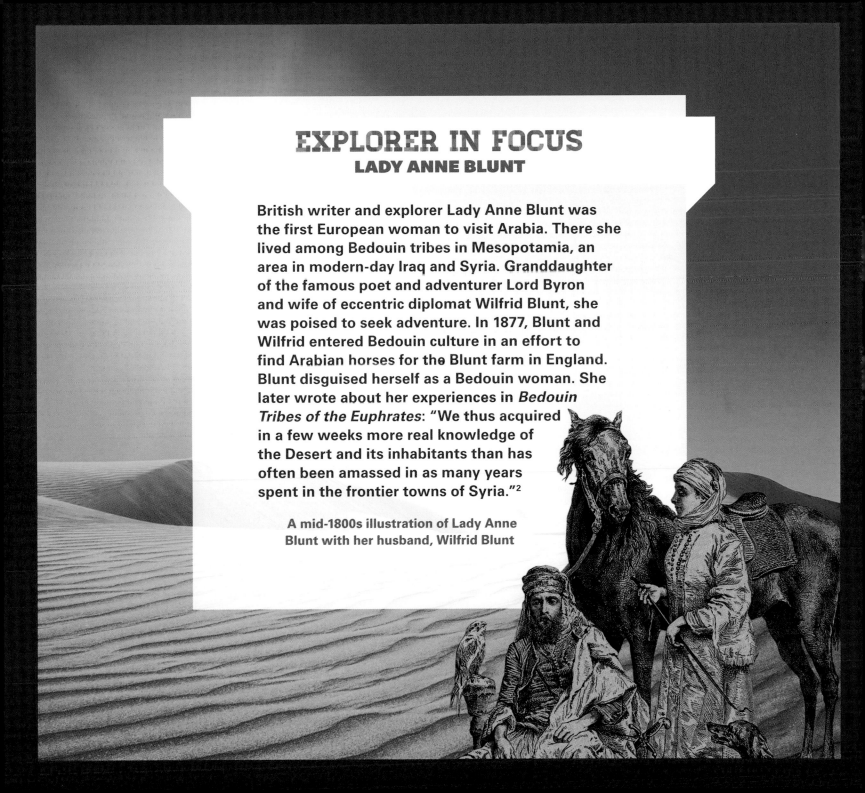

EXPLORER IN FOCUS
LADY ANNE BLUNT

British writer and explorer Lady Anne Blunt was the first European woman to visit Arabia. There she lived among Bedouin tribes in Mesopotamia, an area in modern-day Iraq and Syria. Granddaughter of the famous poet and adventurer Lord Byron and wife of eccentric diplomat Wilfrid Blunt, she was poised to seek adventure. In 1877, Blunt and Wilfrid entered Bedouin culture in an effort to find Arabian horses for the Blunt farm in England. Blunt disguised herself as a Bedouin woman. She later wrote about her experiences in *Bedouin Tribes of the Euphrates*: "We thus acquired in a few weeks more real knowledge of the Desert and its inhabitants than has often been amassed in as many years spent in the frontier towns of Syria."[2]

A mid-1800s illustration of Lady Anne Blunt with her husband, Wilfrid Blunt

the desert city of Damascus, which is the capital of Syria and sits in a desert oasis:

> From his high perch, one sees before him and below him, a wall of dreary mountains, shorn of vegetation, glaring fiercely in the sun; it fences in a level desert of yellow sand, smooth as velvet and threaded far away with fine lines that stand for roads, and dotted with creeping mites we know are camel trains and journeying men; right in the midst of the desert is spread a billowy expanse of green foliage; and nestling in its heart sits the great white city, like an island of pearls and opals gleaming out of a sea of emerald.[3]

Twain eventually published his letters in a book titled *The Innocents Abroad*, which became

DESERT OASES

Oases are fertile green areas that dot otherwise dry and desolate desert areas. They form where groundwater rises to the surface in the form of springs or seeps. Desert people often live in oases, where water is plentiful and crops such as date palms flourish. Oases are a desert explorer's paradise and safety net.

Mark Twain was born
Samuel Langhorne Clemens.
He used Mark Twain as his
pen name when he wrote,
and it became the name he
was most often referred
to as and is remembered
by today.

MARK TWAIN'S TRAVEL ACCOUNTS

US author Mark Twain published *The Innocents Abroad* in 1869. The book describes his travels to the deserts of the Holy Land in the Middle East, as well as his time in Europe, from the perspective of a tourist, or "innocent."[4] The book was popular, selling almost 70,000 copies in the first year and launching Twain's book writing career.[5]

In 1872, Twain published *Roughing It*, a memoir about his 1861 trip through the deserts of Nevada and California. Twain's accounts of this desert trip are less romantic:

The alkali dust cut through our lips. It persecuted our eyes, it ate through the delicate membranes and made our noses bleed and kept them bleeding—and truly and seriously the romance all faded far away and disappeared, and left the desert trip nothing but a harsh reality.[6]

Over the next 30 years, Twain wrote several novels and three more travel books: *A Tramp Abroad, Life on the Mississippi,* and *Following the Equator.* His travel books were always best sellers.

the best-selling travel book of the century. A large number of Americans and Europeans began traveling for pleasure during the Tourist Age. As Twain had done with words, photographers and artists also captured the desert's beauty in their works.

DESERT PHOTOGRAPHY

Modern photography was invented in the 1830s. Into the 1860s, cameras were not typical household items but were owned primarily by professional photographers. Photographers who traveled to capture events or places often published reproductions of their work in books or newspapers. These early images allowed people to view parts of the world they had never seen before.

Pascal Sebah and his son J. Pascal Sebah were influential photographers who revealed new realms of North African deserts to the worldwide public in the 1800s. Another influential desert photographer was US photographer Timothy O'Sullivan. He was instrumental in introducing US citizens to his nation's desert beauty. O'Sullivan applied his photography skills to the Fortieth Parallel Survey, a US government expedition sent to map uncharted areas west of the Mississippi River from 1867 to 1869. In the early 1870s, O'Sullivan joined other expeditions in the western United States and photographed

PASCAL SEBAH: DOCUMENTING THE DESERT

Pascal Sebah was a famous desert photographer in the 1800s. He was from Constantinople, the capital of the Ottoman Empire. Sebah's careful posing of subjects and his lighting techniques made his photographs popular. He opened a studio in Cairo, Egypt, where he documented the people and landscapes of the desert. In 1878, Sebah won a medal for his photographs of Nubian desert tribes. After his death, Pascal's son, J. Pascal Sebah, took over the business. He became the photographer to the sultan and took pictures of desert life all across North Africa and elsewhere in the Ottoman Empire.

Timothy O'Sullivan's
photograph of Canyon de
Chelly in Arizona

several powerful images of desert landscapes. To capture images of the desert at the most dramatic angles, O'Sullivan risked descending steep desert canyons and climbing desert mountains. The images he captured introduced many Americans to spectacular desert landscapes for the first time. One of O'Sullivan's most famous desert images is of an ancient Native American home in Canyon de Chelly in Arizona. Western US deserts captured people's attention in print around this time as well.

DESERT PULP WESTERNS

In the early 1900s, the United States was becoming more industrialized. Some people longed for simpler times of days gone by, and many of them found it by reading a new type of book: the pulp western. Pulp westerns were cheap novels whose pages were filled with gripping and romantic tales of hardship and glory in the desert landscapes of the western United States. Most of the stories took place in the 1800s, when Americans were first settling in the West. Writers of pulp westerns, some of whom had never even been to the western United States, romanticized life in the deserts of the old Wild West. Their action-packed stories, filled with exaggerated tales of real and fictional heroes and heroines, captivated readers throughout the country.

Zane Grey was one of the most popular writers of stories about cowboys, American Indians, explorers, and homesteaders in the American West. His novels, including the 1912 *Riders of the Purple Sage*, were long but full of adventure and romance. Grey gathered material for his books by interviewing people who had lived through the days of the Wild West. Other early pulp western writers include Clarence E. Mulford, who created characters that would soon become Hollywood legends, such as Hopalong Cassidy, and Maxwell Brand, who wrote approximately 530 pulp western novels.[7]

Clarence E. Mulford's famous Hopalong Cassidy character starred in several pulp westerns set in the desert.

THE WESTERN: DESERTS IN FILM

In the first decade of the 1900s, silent movies came into being. Directors wanted to capitalize on the popularity of pulp westerns and drew some of their material from "the fathers of twentieth century western literature," meaning Grey, Brand, and Mulford.[8] In 1910, approximately one-fifth of all Hollywood releases were about the West, and "the Western" movie genre was born.[9]

DESERT'S FIRST FILMS

One of the first widely popular films that was ever made features a desert setting. *The Great Train Robbery* was released in 1903 and was the first film to have an actual plot. The 12-minute film features a gang robbing a train in what is depicted as the Red Desert of Wyoming. But the movie was not actually filmed in the desert. It was filmed in New Jersey on a lot made to resemble the desert.

In the early days of the film industry in Hollywood, California, many films were made to appear as though filmed in the desert, often in the Sahara, but they were actually filmed in Hollywood. These include the silent films *Cleopatra* (1917), *One Arabian Night* (1920), and *The Sheik* (1921). The portrayal of desert people in many of these early films is not very accurate, but the intrigue of desert cultures, which were at the time largely unknown to outsiders, provided great escape for viewers and captivated audiences.

HERITAGE OF THE DESERT

Western films based in the desert were popular throughout the first few decades of the 1900s, including the 1932 film *The Heritage of the Desert*, one of many films inspired by Zane Grey's novels.

Filmmakers must prepare for extreme environments when shooting in the desert, but capturing the vast beauty of the landscape is often worth the trouble.

The plots were always action packed and usually revolved around cowboys, American Indians, and men saving women in distress.

Movie companies with large film crews and budgets sometimes camped out in the scenic deserts of Arizona, Nevada, Utah, and Wyoming to film the movies. Filming the desert landscape became an art of its own. To make a barren scene look picturesque, early filmmakers had to explore new ways to angle the camera. They had to learn how to best position landmarks, such as rock formations, in the shot. New technology allowed filmmakers to reveal desert landscapes to the public, inciting interest and awe. And more discoveries were waiting to be uncovered.

DESERT ARCHITECTURE

Arizona's Grand Canyon, with its colorful rock layers, is one of North America's natural wonders. It is part of a region sometimes called the Painted Desert. The Grand Canyon's natural beauty inspired the work of architect Mary Elizabeth Jane Colter in the early 1900s. Colter's first building, Hopi House, opened in 1905 at the Grand Canyon. She went on to design several other canyon buildings over many years, including both Hermit's Rest and Lookout Studio (1914), Phantom Ranch (1922), Indian Watchtower at Desert View (1932), and Bright Angel Lodge (1935). Hermit's Rest and Lookout Studio showcased a new style of architecture called rustic, which blends into the natural environment. Later architects adopted Colter's rustic style for buildings in national parks throughout the United States.

Several mummies were discovered in a Bahariya oasis tomb in Egypt's Western Desert in 2001. One mummy unearthed was decorated with 100 small gold objects, which, although a common find within mummy tombs, was a great number.

CHAPTER 5

ANCIENT BOOKS AND BODIES: DESERT ARCHAEOLOGY

Deserts hold some of the world's greatest archaeological treasures. The dry air preserves everything from books to bodies. From ancient tools and pottery to handwritten books and pieces of art, each bit of material archaeologists discover weaves together a representation of how people lived during a given time period.

By the early 1900s, desert areas worldwide exploded with archaeological exploration activity. The United

Kingdom opened up its large empire of foreign lands to Westerners, who were hungry to uncover hidden antiquities. At the same time, archaeology was also turning into more of a science than an amateur pastime. Advances in methods for dating the age of a discovery gave archaeologist more credibility. The discoveries being unearthed revealed much about ancient desert history.

THE SILK ROAD

The Silk Road is a 4,000-mile (6,400 km) ancient trade route that once linked two very large and different civilizations, China and Rome.[1] It gets its name from one of the most common items brought by caravan from China, silk. In exchange, Romans sent wool, gold, and silver to the Chinese. The route was important for trading not only goods but also ideas. The road began in Xi'an, China, and ended at the Mediterranean Sea. Traders followed the road through all types of terrain, from the edges of the Takla Makan desert in China through mountains and valleys. If the route around the Takla Makan was impassable because of warfare or political unrest, traders could cut across the desert.

THE CAVES OF THE THOUSAND BUDDHAS

For 1,000 years, beginning in the mid-300s CE, the town of Dunhuang in China's Takla Makan desert was a thriving Buddhist community. It was also a stopping point along the Silk Road, an ancient trade route that connected Asia with Europe and parts of North Africa. Near the town of Dunhuang were the Mogao

Statues are seen tucked within just a portion of the caves that make up the Caves of the Thousand Buddhas in China.

Caves, a labyrinth of 492 caves covering 484,376 square feet (45,000 sq m) that the Chinese call the Caves of the Thousand Buddhas.[2] Over the centuries, Buddhist priests and pilgrims built temples in the caves and decorated them with frescoes and many Buddha statues. In the 1000s, Buddhist monks took some of their greatest written treasures, along with scriptures from other religions, and sealed them in a secret cell of one of the caves to protect them from raiding nomads. In 1900, a Taoist monk discovered the cell and its thousands of ancient Buddhist manuscripts. The writings and silk paintings were still in good condition, thanks to the arid desert climate and the cool, dark caves protecting them from the sun and other elements.

Between 1900 and 1901, Hungarian-born British archaeologist Marc Aurel Stein excavated areas along the Takla Makan. Beneath the sand he found evidence of ancient towns and some ancient wooden tablets with writing on them. On a later expedition, in 1907, Stein advanced along the Great Wall to Dunhuang. The explorer could hardly believe his eyes when he entered the Mogao Caves. Within the caves, Stein saw 400 shrines and temples decorated with 1,000 years' worth of art, artifacts, and scrolls. Among

A page from the Diamond Sutra, found in the Mogao Caves

Stein's finds was the Diamond Sutra, a sacred book of
Buddhist scripture written in 868. The book is considered
one of the world's greatest archaeological finds. It is the
oldest book ever found preserved in its entirety.

Stein was the first European to see the Caves of the Thousand Buddhas. His work helped to piece together the history of central Asia. News of his find also set off a 20-year-long international race to rob the Buddhist artifacts from the Chinese—which Stein himself initiated. After making secret arrangements with the monk in charge of the caves, Stein smuggled dozens of cases full of artifacts out of the caves and sent them to the British Museum in London. It was common practice at that time for European archaeologists to send their finds back home to a European museum. As the century progressed, robberies of desert artifacts continued.

MESOPOTAMIAN ARTIFACTS

After World War I (1914–1918), archaeologists came to the desert regions of Iraq to dig for ancient artifacts left behind from Mesopotamia, a region of present-day Iraq where some of the world's earliest civilizations developed. In

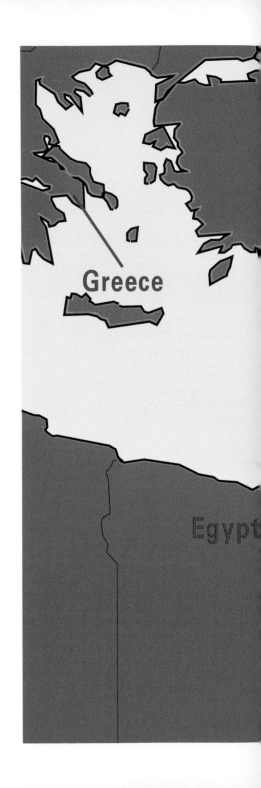

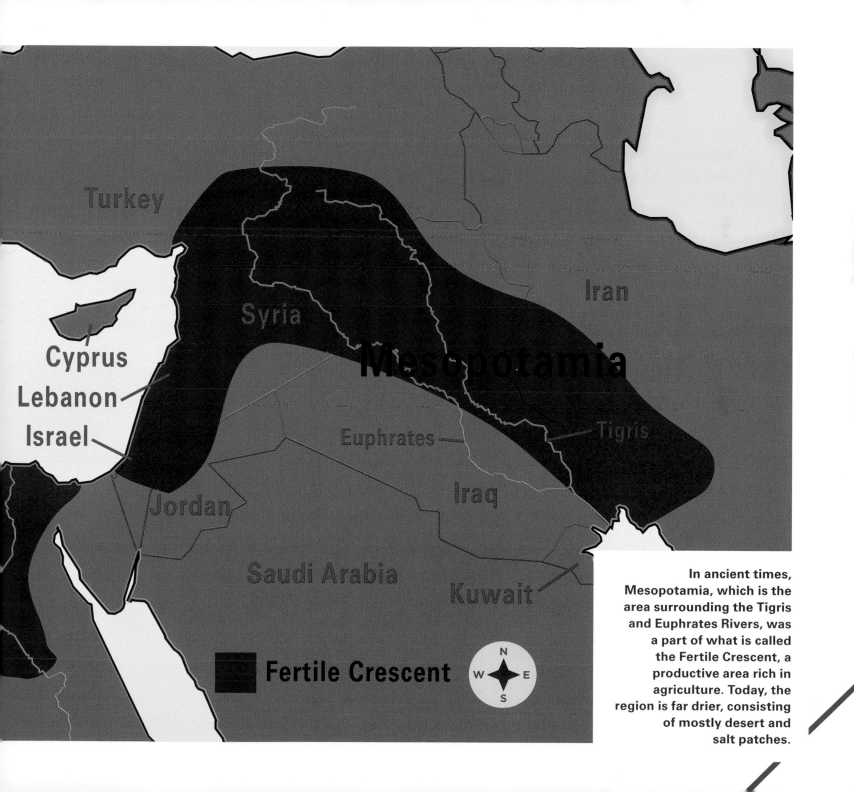

Turkey

Cyprus

Lebanon

Israel

Syria

Mesopotamia

Iran

Euphrates

Tigris

Jordan

Iraq

Saudi Arabia

Kuwait

Fertile Crescent

N W E S

In ancient times, Mesopotamia, which is the area surrounding the Tigris and Euphrates Rivers, was a part of what is called the Fertile Crescent, a productive area rich in agriculture. Today, the region is far drier, consisting of mostly desert and salt patches.

GERTRUDE BELL: A CROWNLESS QUEEN

Gertrude Bell was born in 1868 in the United Kingdom but spent most of her adult life in what is now Iraq. Bell often traveled alone in the Middle East. She spoke Arabic, traveled by camel and horseback through dangerous lands, and risked death and robbery—a bold lifestyle for a Victorian woman.

In Iraq, Bell was a writer, spy, explorer, archaeologist, political administrator and adviser, and director of antiquities. Bell wrote books, drew maps, and compiled reports that helped the British defeat Turkish troops in Iraq during World War I (1914–1918). After the war, she helped to create the borders of modern-day Iraq. As oriental secretary, the only woman at the time to have ever held this important position, Bell was considered the most powerful woman in the British Empire. She played such a large role in creating the modern state of Iraq and spent so much time consulting kings, she was sometimes referred to as the "uncrowned queen of Iraq."[3]

the ruins of Ur, a prominent city-state in Mesopotamia, British archaeologist Leonard Woolley found evidence of an early urban culture, including clay tablets with writing and bronze statues.

In 1922, Gertrude Bell, a British archaeologist and political adviser in the Middle East, began claiming first rights to Mesopotamian artifacts found in Iraq. Under the authority of the Iraqi government, any artifacts Bell claimed were to stay in the country. In 1926, the Iraqi government housed the items in the newly established Baghdad Antiquities Museum, later renamed the National Museum of Iraq. Bell became its director.

The museum contained some of the world's oldest and most treasured artifacts from Mesopotamia. Farther west, in Egypt, exploring for treasuries of another kind—mummies and their riches—was in full force.

THE VALLEY OF THE KINGS

In present-day Luxor, Egypt, once stood Thebes, the capital of the ancient Egyptian empire. Thebes spanned either side of the Nile River. Most people lived on the east side of the river. The west side was the necropolis, or city of the dead. In West Thebes, leaders entombed the mummified bodies of their pharaohs, queens, and high priests with riches for the afterlife.

Leading up to 1922, Egyptologists had discovered 62 tombs in West Thebes in a section they called the Valley of the Kings. All the tombs were empty. Although they were well hidden, the tombs had been robbed, most likely in ancient times. Egyptian writings describe harsh punishments handed out to thieves who were caught. When ancient Greek writer Diodorus Siculus visited the tombs in

The Valley of the Kings is surrounded by vast desert peaks and faces on the Nile River's West Bank.

60 BCE, he wrote, "We found nothing there except the results of pillage and destruction."[4] In 1922, Egyptologist Howard Carter made one of the most important archaeological discoveries of all time in the Valley of the Kings. He unearthed the almost completely intact tomb of King Tut, a short-lived Egyptian pharaoh whose treasures still intrigue the world. Discoveries above ground continued inspiring desert exploration as well.

VALLEY OF THE KINGS TOMB KV63

In 2005, a team led by American Egyptologist Otto Schaden found another tomb in the Valley of the Kings—the first tomb to be discovered since archaeologist Howard Carter found King Tut's tomb in 1922. The tomb was discovered 50 feet (15 m) from King Tut's tomb.[5] It was not full of treasures, and it did not have a body. But it did contain some artifacts that had been preserved, including flowers and linens. The tomb was given the name KV63: *KV* stands for "King's Valley," and *63* stands for the tomb number in the order in which it was discovered.[6]

MISSION IN FOCUS
UNEARTHING KING TUT

In 1922, after eight years of digging through the Valley of the Kings, Howard Carter struck gold both figuratively and literally. The tomb he and his team unearthed showed an unbroken ancient Egyptian seal.

Carter could hardly believe what he saw when he looked inside: gold, jewelry, chests, vases, chariots, statues, and more gold. This was a surprising amount of riches to have been buried with such a young and short-lived pharaoh. King Tut was nine when he became pharaoh of Egypt in 1333 BCE and just 19 when he died.

Carter's find was incredible, but the tomb was not completely intact. Although the ancient Egyptian seal was unbroken, the tomb showed signs of somehow being broken into before. Many items in the tomb were in disarray. Carter also noticed a lack of metalwork, bedding, and glass—items typically buried with royals. Most important, workers had repaired a significant hole in the tomb doorway that was most likely used by thieves. This ancient repair work was proof that the break-ins occurred a long time ago, possibly even shortly after it was sealed, according to some experts.

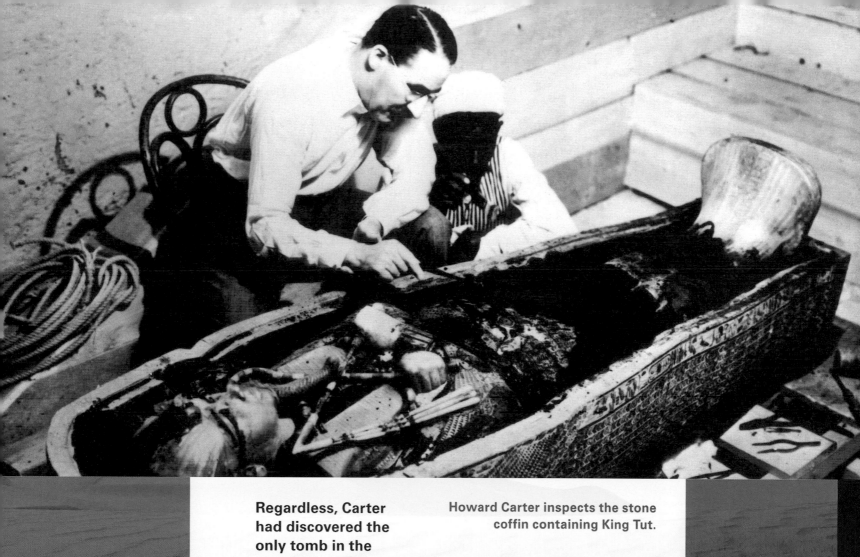

Regardless, Carter had discovered the only tomb in the Valley of the Kings that had not had all its contents stolen or moved. He spent the following ten years cataloging and removing the tomb's items, which totaled more than 5,000 treasures.[7]

Howard Carter inspects the stone coffin containing King Tut.

A Citroën caterpillar that was used to cross the Sahara in 1922 and 1923 sits on display in a Paris, France, museum.

CHAPTER 6

DESERT VEHICLES

In the early 1900s, cars and motorcycles began replacing horses as a primary means of transportation in the United States and elsewhere. For some explorers in the deserts of Africa and central Asia, motorized vehicles began replacing the camel.

CATERPILLARS

One such mode of motorized transport was a French Citroën caterpillar, also known as a half-track. The vehicle had two wheels in front and rubber belts on the rear axles. André Citroën, a French automotive engineer and manufacturer, designed the vehicle to traverse difficult terrain such as sand. His hope was the French government would find the vehicle useful in crossing the terrain of the French colonies in Africa. The Citroën caterpillar was the most modern all-terrain vehicle in the 1920s and 1930s.

One of the first to use a caterpillar in the desert was Prince Kemal El Din Ibn Hussein of Egypt. In the early 1900s, Prince Kemal had an opportunity to become king of Egypt after his father died. The prince, however, turned it down for what he considered to be more exciting adventures: he wanted to explore the desert. One of Kemal's goals was to cross the Great Sand Sea—the third-largest field of dunes in the world—located in the

THE GREAT SAND SEA

The Great Sand Sea is a large field of sand dunes in western Egypt and eastern Libya. Shaped by strong winds that blow across the Sahara, the Great Sand Sea contains hundreds of dune ridges. The area stretches 57,915 square miles (150,000 sq km), creating for those that explore it the sense of being in the middle of an ocean of sand, or a sand sea.[1] The dunes' loose sand makes them difficult to cross—whether by foot, on camel or horse, or in a vehicle. Dunes have been measured as long as 86 miles (140 km).[2] Sand seas or ergs occur in all major desert areas, as well as on Mars. The Rub' al-Khali in Saudi Arabia is the largest sand sea on Earth at 250,000 sq miles (650,000 sq km).[3] The pristine dunes of the Namib Sand Sea in southwestern Africa are up to 1,200 feet (370 m) high.[4]

northern Sahara. Between 1923 and 1926, Kemal set off on several desert expeditions using the caterpillar.

Similar to many other expeditions in the Sahara, Prince Kemal and his group of explorers began some of their adventures in the Kharga, an oasis located along the northern portion of the ancient Forty Days' Road trade route that had a guaranteed water supply. The group headed westward until it reached the edge of the Great Sand Sea.

According to C. S. Jarvis, a traveling companion and fellow explorer, the caterpillar, while more efficient than a car for traveling in the desert, did have its share of issues. One was the vehicle's radiator, which needed a lot of one of their most precious resources—water. As Jarvis explained of the caterpillars,

> They were the last word in desert transport in those days, as they would climb any sand-dune and, despite the small size of their engines, could develop enough power to drag another car out of the sand. But they had two great disadvantages—they could never travel faster than fifteen miles an hour even in good going,

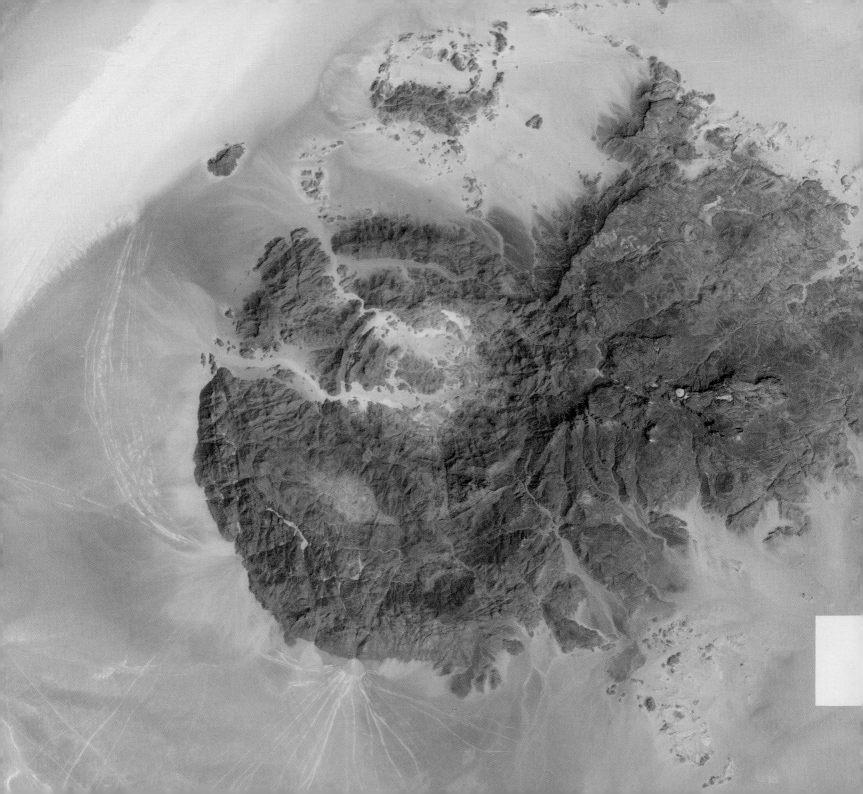

and their cooling apparatus was not up to the heat developed by the engine, so that they consumed vast quantities of water.[5]

According to Prince Kemal, the caterpillar proved worthless in the seemingly endless expanse of dunes. Although he did not penetrate the Great Sand Sea, Prince Kemal did reach and name the Gilf Kebir, a sandstone plateau also known as the Great Wall. His team also created a detailed map of Jebel Uweinat, a mountain range in the Sahara, located where the borders of Egypt, Sudan, and Libya meet.

In November 1929, British army officer, geologist, and explorer Ralph Bagnold would try the same feat over the Great Sand Sea using a different vehicle—a Ford Model T.

FORGING THROUGH THE DESERT IN FORDS

Through 1927, many explorers chose Henry Ford's Model T for desert travel. Although it had narrow tires, the Model T

A NASA satellite image shows the Jebel Uweinat from space.

was lightweight, had high ground clearance, and could travel five times faster than a camel.[6] To avoid getting stuck in soft sand, drivers needed to keep the heavy car moving at speeds of up to 40 miles per hour (64 kmh).[7] If the Model T slowed down to 19 miles per hour (31 kmh) or less, the tires sank into, rather than skimmed over, the sand, stalling the vehicle.[8] In 1927, Ford discontinued production of the Model T and replaced it with the Model A—another favorite among desert travelers. With better brakes, newly designed axles, and the addition of shock absorbers, the Model A also performed well in the desert.

Between 1926 and 1929, Bagnold was stationed in Egypt. During this time, he sold his small English car to buy a more reliable desert vehicle—a Model T. Bagnold's goal was to travel westward, deep into the Sahara to map and explore. Bagnold was fascinated by the desert. He thoroughly enjoyed the thrill of maneuvering over sometimes-difficult sands, as well as "the clean coolness of sand dunes in the

Vintage Model T's follow the Caborca-Yuma trail in 1997, which is a road in the Arizona desert that explorers traveled in 1915 using the same vehicle.

DESERT SOUNDS DURING EXPEDITIONS

Many explorers, including Ralph Bagnold, have reported hearing strange sounds in the desert. In the still of the night, after a windy day, the dunes suddenly manifest a penetrating, low-pitched sound like that of someone playing the drums or musical instruments. The sound is too loud to speak over. Marco Polo, who traveled the Silk Road in the 1200s, believed evil desert spirits caused the sounds.

Scientists attributed the sounds to avalanches, but no one knew exactly why the movement of sand made the noises. Using sophisticated equipment, researcher Bruno Andreotti from the University of Paris explored the desert phenomenon in 2002. He learned that avalanches produce surface waves, which act like a loudspeaker. The grains of sand collide at nearly 100 times per second. The surface waves synchronize the collisions, so they are all on the same beat, creating a loud rhythmic sound that can last for up to 15 minutes.[10]

evening, and the dry sparkling desert air."[9]

Bagnold also used Model As. In 1929, Bagnold and five fellow explorers set out with Model As to penetrate the Great Sand Sea. During the trip, Bagnold made several important discoveries that made traveling deep into the desert by car doable and somewhat safe. First, he refined the sun compass, which uses the sun to help people navigate in a desert without landmarks. Next, he discovered a simple method for dislodging cars stuck in the sand and then improved the design of the car's radiator so that it would not lose so much water.

Bagnold's expedition also discovered a simple but novel way to create sand tracks. They created steel channels out of flat metal pieces five feet (1.5 m) long and 11 inches (28 cm) wide used for roofing that they found in a Cairo junkyard. First, the men scooped out the sand from the front of each rear wheel of the stuck vehicle and then placed the channels in the man-made depressions and tucked them slightly underneath the tires. When the driver pulled forward, the tires had a solid surface and the needed traction to dislodge from soft sand.

When the explorers reached the Great Sand Sea, they increased their speed to 37 miles per hour (60 kmh) and found themselves ascending a dune. Bagnold described the magic he experienced when traveling up the first dune:

> *A huge glaring wall of yellow shot up high into the sky a yard in front of us. The [truck] tipped violently backwards—and we rose as in a lift, smoothly without vibration. We floated up and up on a yellow cloud.*[11]

Ralph Bagnold in 1929

They had entered the Great Sand Sea and had not sunk in the sand. They instead found themselves 100 feet (30 m) aboveground atop the dune.

Bagnold and his team proved cars could traverse even the toughest desert sands successfully. In 1932, he set out with eight others and became the first to cross the Libyan Desert from east to west in a car—a 5,000-mile (8,050 km) journey.[12] Bagnold is remembered for leading the Long Range Desert Group, a patrol of Allied troops, through the Sahara during World War II (1939–1945) to distract Italian forces. His vast knowledge of the desert proved invaluable to British forces. In 1941, he published *Physics of Blown Sand and Desert Dunes*, a book on sediment transport, or the movement of sand, silt, and dust. Although he wrote the material more than 70 years ago, scientists today still rely on Bagnold's observations.

CROSSING ASIA ON HALF-TRACKS

As Bagnold traversed African deserts, others were exploring Asia's deserts. In 1931, French industrialist and explorer Citroën had already completed an expedition across Africa, including its deserts, in his Citroën caterpillars when he began planning a trek across Asia. Citroën planned to trek from Beirut, Lebanon, to Peking, China, which is the present-day city of Beijing. This path would take him across the Gobi and Arabian Deserts. For the expedition, Citroën and his crew of archaeologists, scientists, mechanics, photographers, and cinematographers would bring 14 caterpillars, which they would use to cross not only hot and cold deserts but also treacherous mountain passes. But difficult terrain was not their only challenge. The lands they would traverse were also torn by war. At the time, Russia had claimed parts of central Asia and formed a new country called the Soviet Union, and China was going through a civil war.

In April 1931, Citroën split his group in two to ensure that at least one of them made it through areas undergoing political unrest. One group left Beirut for the Pamirs, a mountainous region located mostly in Tajikistan. The other group would start in Peking, traverse the Gobi Desert, and meet the Pamir group in the Xinjiang region

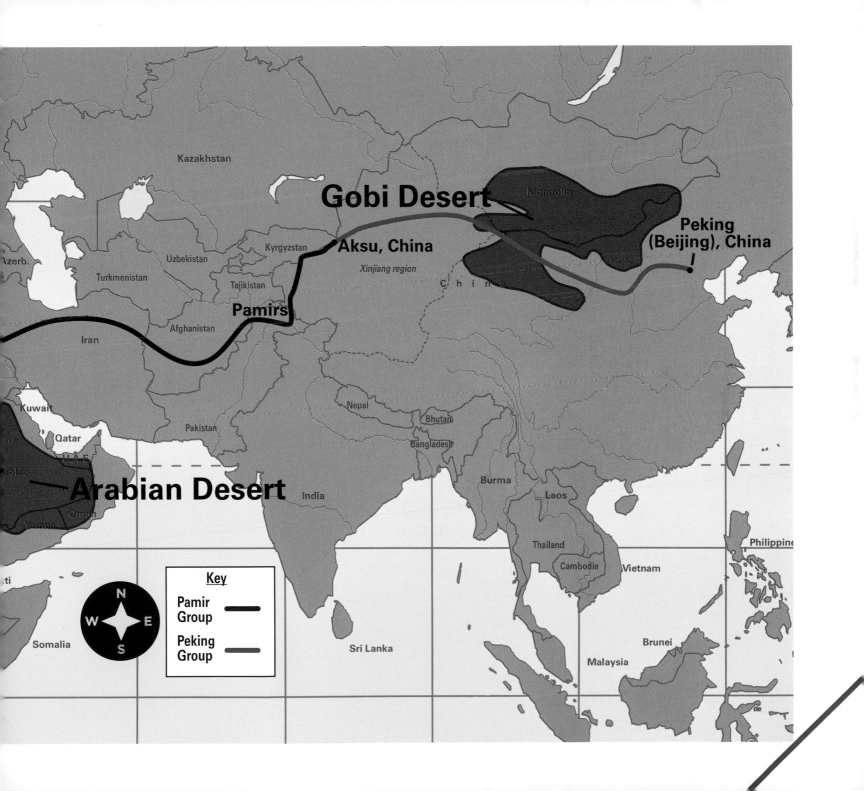

Gobi Desert

Aksu, China

Xinjiang region

Pamirs

Peking
(Beijing), China

Arabian Desert

Kazakhstan

Mongolia

Uzbekistan

Kyrgyzstan

Turkmenistan

Tajikistan

Afghanistan

China

Iran

Nepal

Bhutan

Kuwait

Bangladesh

Qatar

Pakistan

Somalia

India

Sri Lanka

Burma

Laos

Thailand

Cambodia

Vietnam

Philippine

Brunei

Malaysia

Azerb.

U.A.E.

Oman

Yemen

Key

Pamir
Group ——

Peking
Group ——

N
W   E
S

in China. The two groups planned to then return together to Peking at trip's end.

The Pamir group passed through the deserts of Syria, Iraq, Iran, and Afghanistan, often suffering the burning heat. Once they reached the mountains, they had to take their vehicles apart in order to get through the narrow passes and then reassemble them. Eventually, the team gave up on the caterpillars and relied on horses and yaks.

The Peking group became held up in northwestern China. The Chinese governor would not permit them to leave. They finally met up with the Pamir group in Aksu, China, on October 8, 1931—after giving the governor three of their vehicles. On November 30, the entire group began crossing the deserts and mountains of southern Mongolia and northern China in frighteningly cold temperatures, minus 22 degrees Fahrenheit (−30°C).[13]

Photographer Maynard Owen Williams wrote about some of the hardships the expedition faced on the last 2,000 miles (3,200 km) of the journey:

One of Citroën's groups crossing the Yellow River, today called the Hoang Ho River, in northern China with their caterpillar in January 1932

Two of our caravans had been pillaged. The rebel
Ma Chung Ying stood astride the Great Road waiting
for us, with tons of our supplies already in his hands.
Sand dune and river, desert and rocky defile lay
across our path. The cold of the Mongolian plateau
was often in our thoughts. . . . [We had] great

admiration for the mechanics, toiling with bare hands
in the dead of the winter night.[14]

The group finally reached Peking on February 12, 1932, haggard and frostbitten. In the years that followed, caterpillars and cars would continue to be used for desert travel, sometimes at great expense to the desert environment.

THE DOWNSIDE OF DESERT VEHICLES

The caterpillar has been replaced by more advanced vehicles, such as the Jeep, the Land Rover, and elaborate military 4x4 trucks made specifically for high-speed desert travel. Some explorers have used motorcycles to cross deserts, including a more recent expedition in 1999, when adventurers Michael Martin and Elke Wallner set out to explore five continents' worth of deserts in 900 days on a motorcycle. All these vehicles have made deserts more accessible, including to tourists. But there are downsides to this type of travel as well. Motorized vehicles can cause damage to desert environments by tearing up terrain.

Fuel use can also cause pollution. Finding ways to travel without creating environmental damage is an ongoing task for all types of transportation used by researchers and scientists worldwide.

DAMAGING DESERT TOURISM: DUNE BASHING

Although motorized vehicle travel can cause damage to desert environments and wildlife, tourism companies advertise the fun of riding through the desert. A sport called "dune bashing" is popular in the United Arab Emirates, where riders maneuver through the tall dunes of Lima, in the Sechura desert, at high speeds, "bashing" the dunes for a roller-coaster ride effect. In the process, they damage desert plants and wildlife habitat, including animal living spaces and breeding grounds, which for reptiles and insects are often under the sand.

MISSION IN FOCUS
CROSSING THE WORLD'S DESERTS IN 900 DAYS

In 1999, photographer Michael Martin set out on a years-long desert expedition. He and filmmaker Elke Wallner prepared to travel deserts across five continents by motorcycle in 900 days to promote travel and capture unique desert photos. Martin, as described on his Web site, "likes to cover all his journeys by motorbike, riding over desolate rocky mountains and through hour-long sandstorms, in the bitter cold and stifling heat, over mined out slopes such as in Afghanistan or in the rebel regions of Chad or Ethiopia."[15] He and Wallner first embarked on their lengthy motorcycle trip from their home in Munich, Germany. Overall, Martin and Wallner traveled to five continents and 50 countries before finally finishing their trip in Egypt in the Sahara. The pair documented the ups and downs of their long journey, capturing the remarkable desert landscapes and the desert

people they
got to know on
their travels. The
compilation of their journey was used to create
their documentary *Exploring the Deserts of the
Earth: 5 Continents, 50 Countries, 900 Days.*

Michael Martin rode around the world
on a motorcycle similar to this BMW.

Bones and teeth are among the most common fossils discovered, but ancient foot, skin, or body imprints are also considered a type of fossil.

CHAPTER 7

DINOSAUR DIGS

Deserts are natural laboratories for paleontologists. Fossils consist of remains or traces, such as bones or leaf imprints, of plant and animal life preserved in the earth's crust. These fossils can be millions of years old. They help scientists piece together the history of life on Earth.

Paleontologists have discovered a large number of fossils in the deserts of central Asia, Africa, South America, and North America. Deserts are the perfect environment for fossil exploration because of their sparse vegetation and thin soil, which exposes large expanses of ancient rock where many fossils are embedded. The dry desert air also protects the fossils from decaying.

Although fossils are found in abundance across deserts and elsewhere, less than 1 percent of all living organisms over time become fossilized.[1] Most fossils come from humans or animals that had a solid skeleton, such as dinosaurs.

DINOSAUR DIGS

Dinosaurs lived on Earth for approximately 180 million years. Common belief is that they first appeared approximately 245 million years ago and died out approximately 66 million years ago, at the end of the Cretaceous period.

Hunting for dinosaur bones is a relatively new science. Before the mid-1800s, people did not even know dinosaurs once existed. Some may have stumbled across dinosaur remains, but no documentation exists to prove they understood what they were. In some cases, these unexplained bones are thought to have inspired mythical creatures in stories and art.

In 1842, British anatomist Richard Owen noticed the giant fossil remains of three different reptiles found in southern England were unlike the remains of other reptiles—they were very large, had five instead of two vertebrae, and their limbs did not sprawl out to the side, similar to other lizards, but were upright. Owen introduced the term *Dinosauria* to identify the giant fossil remains, and a new study was born. Although paleontologists have since learned a lot about dinosaurs, many questions are yet unanswered. Scientists continue exploring the world's deserts for fossils, searching for clues about ancient life on Earth.

MYSTERIOUS FOSSIL CREATURES

The ancient Romans who lived in the deserts of the Middle East and the Mediterranean created many statues of a mythological creature called the griffin. Griffins usually had a lion's body and an eagle's head and sometimes bore wings. The statues were decorative, often placed in front of a building as if to protect it. Some scientists believe the Romans might have created the image of the griffin after piecing together different animal remains—including those of dinosaurs.

A paleontologist unearths a giant dinosaur fossil in the Argentine desert.

CHALLENGES OF DIGGING IN THE DESERT

Paleontologists are scientists at heart and explorers and adventurers by necessity. To find fossils, they sometimes must travel deep into a desert, away from the comforts of home and even hotels. They eat foods they are unaccustomed to, sleep in tents or under the stars, and relieve themselves outdoors. And they need to have a knowledgeable and resourceful crew who can fix a Land Rover with whatever material is on hand, distinguish one desert wadi from another, prevent the expedition from getting lost in the desert, and identify any locals who might be a threat.

Exploring for fossils in the Abu Dhabi Desert of the United Arab Emirates, British geologist Peter Whybrow conveys the conditions scientists in the desert must put up with—and those they appreciate:

No one but a geologist would voluntarily visit this place. In Spring, it can be mind-blastingly hot: walking becomes a plod; breathing is labored and tiny flies seek moisture from nose, eyes, and lips—there is no wind and no shade. On other Spring days . . . a sky of an astonishingly brilliant shade of blue overlies a velvet-like silence, punctuated only by the song of desert larks, and the chattering wings of huge dragonflies.[2]

DINOSAUR GRAVEYARDS OF PATAGONIA

Patagonia is a dry plateau in Argentina. It lies between the Andes Mountains on the west and the Atlantic Ocean on the east. The deserts of Patagonia hold some of the largest dinosaur bones in the world. Paleontologists have actively explored the region for many years and have found so many dinosaur bones the area has been called a "dinosaur graveyard."[3]

Some of the most remarkable finds in the Argentine desert include fossils of the *Argentinosaurus*, thought to be the largest plant-eating dinosaur ever to roam the earth.[4] The animal, which was 115 feet (35 m) long, weighed 88 to 111 short tons (80 to 100 metric tons).[5] It lived approximately 85 million years ago, when it is estimated Patagonia was covered with food in the form of lush plants.

Scientists began finding *Argentinosaurus* fossils in 1987. In 1994, Ruben Carolini, an auto mechanic and amateur fossil hunter, was looking for fossils in Neuquén, a province in Patagonia. Carolini discovered a large, carnivorous dinosaur now called *Giganotosaurus carolinii*. This dinosaur weighed approximately 8 short tons (7.3 metric tons) and measured between 45 and 47 feet (13.7 and 14.3 m) in length.[6] Some believe this dinosaur's features were similar to *Tyrannosaurus rex* but

DINOSAUR CLUES

Paleontologists often rely on volunteers to help scour an area and locate possible fossil remains. The volunteers are trained to look for certain signs. In September 1998, for instance, in the desert badlands of northwestern New Mexico, a volunteer came across what paleontologists call a "surface expression" —a small pile of loose bone fragments. A surface expression is a good clue. It indicates a skeleton most likely lies below the surface. Based on this clue, scientists began excavating. They soon unearthed the remains of a *Tyrannosaurus rex*.

estimate the *Giganotosaurus carolinii* may have been slightly longer and heavier.[7]

Scientists have discovered dinosaur fossils around the world. Another particularly large collection, or graveyard, lies across the globe in Mongolia.

GOBI DESERT DINOSAURS

In Mongolia lies a stretch of the Gobi Desert called Ukhaa Tolgod, or "brown hills." Paleontologists recently unearthed an enormous number of dinosaur fossils in Ukhaa Tolgod, and evidence suggests there is much more to find. During a three-hour period on one particular day in 1993, paleontologists were finding one fossil every three minutes, which is an amazing speed for what is normally a slow and laborious

DINOSAUR-BIRD EVOLUTION

Some paleontologist believe approximately 150 million years ago, a certain group of dinosaurs did not die out but began growing feathers and evolving into birds. These dinosaurs were a diverse group of flesh-eating dinosaurs called theropods. Theropods range in size from the *Microraptor*, which was approximately the size of a crow, to the colossal *Tyrannosaurus rex*. Smaller theropods were long thought to be the ancestors of birds, since they share some common traits. Both theropods and birds have a wishbone, which is a joined clavicle, or collarbone. They also each have short, stiff tails and flexible wrist joints.

process. One of their greatest finds during this excavation were fossils of *Mononychus*, later named *Mononykus*, which is a species that seems to show the transition between dinosaurs and birds.

Tedious work and extreme terrain and climate do not stop paleontologists from excavating desert sites. In fact, dinosaur fossil digs have occurred in some of the world's coldest spots.

FROZEN DESERT FOSSILS

Approximately 95 percent of Antarctica, the largest desert in the world, is covered with a very thick sheet of ice, which is nearly two miles (3.2 km) thick in some spots.[8] Brutally cold temperatures and stormy seas surrounding the island continent have made exploration difficult. But scientists have long believed they can learn much about the earth's climate and history by studying Antarctica. This includes learning through paleontology.

Digging for bones in the coldest desert on Earth has its challenges. Although paleontologists suspect much of

Paleontologists dig for dinosaur fossils on Antarctica's Mount Kirkpatrick in 2004. Similar to other deserts, Antarctica has proven to be a rich site for fossils.

the continent holds a striking number of dinosaur remains, vast regions are inaccessible because of the thick ice covering. Most paleontological searches have taken place on the coasts or high in the mountains, the only places where the ground is not a solid sheet of ice. Time is another issue paleontologists face when excavating Antarctica. The continent experiences six months of darkness each year and has frigid temperatures that become life threatening with extended exposure. These factors limit the number of hours and days researchers can spend outdoors.

Dinosaur remains found on Antarctica are not from the largest or most ferocious species, but they have helped scientists better understand the link between dinosaurs in Antarctica and Australia, which were connected millions of years ago before their tectonic plates drifted apart.

HUMAN FOSSIL FINDS

In 1992, Gen Suwa, a paleontologist from Japan, was combing the desert scrubland of the Afar depression in Ethiopia when he stumbled on an old tooth. An analysis of the tooth showed it was 4.4 million years old. Suwa and other researchers from his team returned to the pebbly desert region and found an additional 125 bone fragments, all belonging to the same creature. Over the following 17 years, the scientists pieced the fossils together to reshape Ardi, a female human ancestor. Given the scientific name *Ardipithecus ramidus*, Ardi measures four feet (1.2 m) tall and weighs 110 pounds (50 kg).[9]

Ardi was an important find for paleontologists. She predates Lucy, another human ancestor fossil found in the Afar depression thought to be 1.2 million years old. Before Ardi, Lucy's human remains were considered the oldest ever found. Studying both Lucy and Ardi has helped scientists understand the earliest phases of human evolution.

FOSSIL FUELS

Not all fossils remain intact as solid remains. Over millions of years, organic plant and animal matter decayed under Earth's surface. Together, this matter became fossil fuels. Fossil fuels are sources of energy. They include coal, petroleum, oil, and natural gas. Deposits of fossil fuels are

Based on the fossils found in the Ethiopian desert, scientists have created depictions of early human ancestor *Ardipithecus ramidus*, or Ardi.

Adding a link

Scientists have discovered the oldest pre-human ancestor found to date, nicknamed "Ardi."

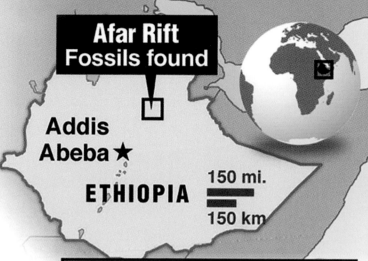

Afar Rift
Fossils found

Addis Abeba ★

ETHIOPIA

150 mi.

150 km

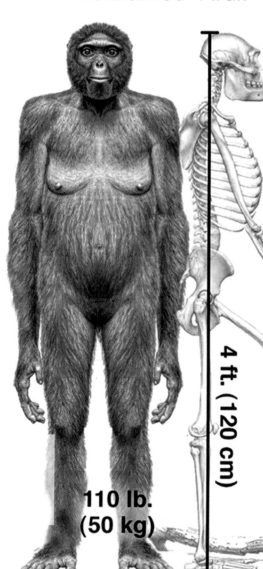

4 ft. (120 cm)

110 lb. (50 kg)

Ardipithecus ramidus

- Hominid species, a pre-human primate
- Lived 4.4 million years ago
- First fossils found in 1992; has taken 17 years to assess their significance

Opposable thumbs

No arched feet
Could not walk or run for long distances

© 2009 MCT

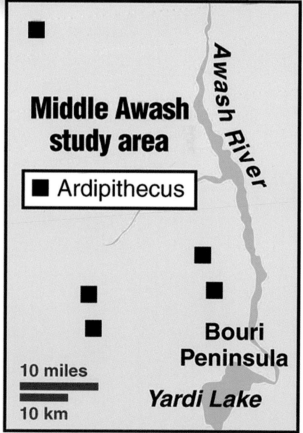

Middle Awash study area

■ Ardipithecus

Awash River

Bouri Peninsula

Yardi Lake

10 miles

10 km

Source: Science, Illustrations by J.H. Matternes
Graphic: Melina Yingling

frequently found near the remains of dinosaurs and other ancient life-forms and are very valuable. Humans have used coal for heating since prehistoric times. In the 1300s, the Hopi Indians of the southwestern United States used it to cook and make pottery. Fossil fuels have provided much of the world's energy in recent centuries. Fossil fuel energy is used to heat homes, power lights, make gasoline, and run factories. Fossil fuels including oil are a limited resource, and once they are used up, they will be gone. This makes oil extremely valuable. Oil is prevalent and easily accessible in Earth's deserts. Controlling oil resources has economically transformed many desert countries, especially in the Middle East, as oil money poured in during the 1900s.

Reaching valuable fossil deposits in the desert has a negative impact on the environment. Drilling causes pollution by expelling carbon into the air, and oil spills hurt plant and animal life. Warfare in oil-rich deserts sets the stage for ecological damage, both accidental and on purpose. Toward the end of the Persian Gulf War (1990–1991), Iraqi troops leaving Kuwait were ordered to

Huge oil pipelines and wells can mar landscape and damage desert ecosystems, as can oil spills and pollution created by the digging machinery.

scorch the earth. They set 800 oil wells on fire, burning an average of 3 to 5 million barrels of oil a day and placing the entire desert ecosystem under threat.[10] Excavating deserts in search of fossil fuels has been a leading cause behind desert exploration. But today, awareness and protection of the environment and desert ecosystems has increased, and explorers and scientists seek ways to make use of desert resources while conserving desert environments.

Astronauts train at the Mars Analog Research Station in Utah, where geologic and biological research, simulated tests, and created habitats provide understanding of how to explore similar desert terrain on Mars.

CHAPTER 8

DESERT EXPLORATION TODAY

Today, many desert plants, animals, and landscapes have been mapped and studied, but researchers and explorers continue making desert discoveries. Although the bulk of desert exploration was completed and maps drafted in the 1800s, future interests inspire further exploration for a variety of reasons. Deserts on Earth are used as simulators and researched to discover more about the surface of Mars, which is a desert. Scientists and economists are

STUDYING DESERTS IN SPACE

The surface of Mars is a desert. To study life on Mars, some researchers have turned to deserts, including the Utah desert and the Atacama in Chile because their climates and landscapes resemble that of Mars. To do this, researchers send a robotic rover that has drills, cameras, and other equipment into the Atacama. The rover can sense where plants, animals, and water exist within the desert. Researchers use the data it collects to understand more about life in extreme environments. The National Aeronautics and Space Administration (NASA) has sent several rovers to Mars. In 2012, NASA sent the rover *Curiosity* to Mars to determine whether the planet's Gale Crater once contained water, which would indicate life might have existed on Mars at some point. By moving slowly across the planet, shooting lasers into rock to analyze the material, and taking thousands of pictures, the rover delivers important data to scientists—some of which shows water once flowed through the Gale Crater.

determining how to collect the desert sun's energy and distribute it worldwide, and city planners are using desert towns as models for green living. Farmers are finding resourceful ways to use deserts to raise food. Engineers are finding new and creative ways to collect water from the desert, in the form of fog. This future stage of desert exploration includes learning how to keep desert ecosystems thriving and desert landscapes intact.

CATCHING DESERT FOG

Squeezed between the Pacific Ocean and the Andes Mountains, the Atacama in South America is the driest place on Earth. More than 1 million people live in this desert.[1] For many of them, water is scarce and expensive. In coastal areas around the world, including deserts such as the Atacama and the Namib, fog often rolls in from the sea and blankets the land. Fog is a source of moisture, and it is offering new hope to people who live in coastal deserts in Africa and South America. With help from international organizations, residents in some Atacama communities have begun capturing water from the winter fogs that last from June to November each year.

How does this work? People set up large nets to capture the vapor, or water droplets, from fog. As the wind blows fog through the nets, the vapor condenses and sticks to the mesh. As more vapor collects, the droplets cluster together into full-size drops. When the drops get big and heavy enough, they slide down the nets into a gutter below. The water moves through these gutters to pipes that carry it to tanks or pools.

The people of Bellavista, a town on the steep slopes outside of Lima, Peru's capital city, were curious about fog catching. Their village was too far from Lima to connect

A man in Bellavista, Peru, stands near a large fog-catching net. Droplets form from fog and drop into a gutter that feeds into a larger container holding the water for irrigation drinking.

to the water supply system. Truck drivers would haul in water and charge more than the residents could afford to pay. In 2006, the town worked hard to build a fog-catching system. Yet even as they lugged heavy bricks and sandbags to build water tanks, they thought the whole idea was a little crazy.

That was before they saw the results. Anne Lummerich, a German biologist who guided the villagers through the project, noted the fog water was so plentiful that it was like "opening a tap."[2] One year later, with the addition of nets with a better design, Bellavista was collecting as much as 600 gallons (2,271 L) of water a day.[3]

The fog water collected in Bellavista provides much-needed water for gardens and trees—both of which yield food that helps stretch the meager incomes of Bellavista's residents. The trees also have another benefit: their leaves act as fog catchers.

More people are moving to the outskirts of Lima in hopes of good jobs and a better life. At the same time, water is becoming even scarcer. As the earth's climate gets hotter, the glaciers in the Andes Mountains are melting away. They have been the main source of water for Lima. Fog catching cannot supply all of Lima with water, but it works well for small communities. A few other villages near Bellavista have begun to collect fog. International development organizations need more funding to bring the system to foggier desert communities around the world, such as in Namibia, Africa.

A FOG-CATCHING BUG

In the Namib desert on Africa's southwestern coast, a beetle inspired scientists to develop better fog-catching materials. The back on Namibian beetles has a rough surface. When early morning fog rolls in from the Atlantic Ocean, the beetles face into the wind and raise their backs, as if doing a handstand. The fog's tiny water droplets stick to raised bumps on the shell. The droplets grow as more of them cling together on each bump. Eventually they get big enough to slide down into waxy grooves on the beetle. The grooves lead directly to the beetle's mouth, supplying it with all the water it needs.

GREEN LIVING IN THE BROWN DESERT

For environmentalists, deserts are the perfect location to test green, or carbon-reduced, living. Most scientists attribute the world's changing climate to carbon gases in the atmosphere that are created by burning fossil fuels such as coal to create electricity. Using power from the sun to provide the world's electricity would prevent a lot of further damage to the environment. Some experts believe deserts could become "the carbon-free power houses of the 21st century."[4] This is largely because of the massive amount of solar energy that can be collected in deserts.

The sunniest place in the world is the eastern Sahara, where the sun shines approximately 4,300 hours a year.[5] Scientists have calculated collecting the sun's energy in

FIRST FOSSIL FUEL–FREE DESERT CITY

The United Arab Emirates (UAE) is a federation of seven territories along the Arabian Peninsula. The UAE is part desert, part mountains, and part wetlands. The UAE's economy is based on oil. Now the federation is gaining a reputation for being a leader in renewable energy.

On February 8, 2008, builders in the desert of the UAE broke ground for the world's first zero-carbon, zero-waste, car-free city. Masdar City, named after the government-owned renewable energy company, is being built in part to help accommodate the area's growing population. When completed near 2025, Masdar City will have enough housing for 40,000 residents and will be the UAE's technology center.[6] The city's buildings are designed using a combination of new and ancient building materials and techniques to ensure the buildings need only a minimal amount of energy to run. The plan is to power Masdar City using only renewable energy sources such as solar power.

a 250,000 square mile (650,000 sq km) area of the Sahara using solar panels could create more than enough energy to supply electricity to every home and business around the world.[7] According to a report by the United Nations, "If the huge, solar-power potential of deserts can be economically harnessed the world has a future free from fossil fuels."[8] In addition to providing massive amounts of solar energy, researchers are exploring how to use an old desert resource, groundwater, for a new type of farming in the desert.

FISH AND SHRIMP FARMS IN THE DESERT

In the Negev desert region of Israel, August temperatures average 97.5 degrees Fahrenheit (36.4°C).[9] Rainfall is low. Despite the extreme heat, resourceful farmers have found a way to raise shrimp and fish in the Negev and other scorching deserts in Arizona and parts of central Asia. Why would farmers want to raise water-dependent animals in some of the driest places on Earth? And where do they get the water?

Several large solar power arrangements have been built in deserts, including at the Red Rock Canyon National Conservation Area in the Mojave Desert in Nevada.

The shrimp and fish being raised are saltwater animals normally found in the oceans. Under the Negev and many other deserts lie aquifers filled with ancient water—water

Postlarvae shrimp, or shrimp that are between hatching and adult stages, are placed in troughs to get them used to fresh water in an Arizona desert shrimp farm.

that might have seeped into the ground thousands of years ago. These aquifers lie approximately 50 to 150 feet (15 to 46 m) below the earth's surface.[10] Farmers drill into the underground waters with large machines similar to those used in oil drilling. They bring the water to the surface and create pools. The water is hot and salty, which are conditions in which shrimp and saltwater fish thrive.

Farms using these techniques raise approximately 30 million short tons (27.2 million metric tons) of fish and shrimp each year.[11] The ancient water supply is a rich natural resource in the desert, but it will not last forever. Experts estimate the underground water supply under the Negev will last only 200 years if farmers continue using it for aquaculture.[12] Researchers are looking into recycling the salty water, which would include first using it in spas, channeling it to fish and shrimp farms, and then using it to water crops.

EFFECTS OF EMPTYING AQUIFERS

Most desert dwellers rely on groundwater to meet their water needs, but aquifers are not endless water supplies. Desert cities that use a lot of water can eventually deplete aquifers. This can cause serious consequences above ground, including costly efforts to pump deeper aquifers and owners abandoning farms for lack of water.

Many desert aquifers contain rainwater that fell thousands of years ago, when the area had a very different climate—wet, not dry. Because deserts receive little rainfall, the groundwater that desert dwellers pump out does not get fully replenished. Large desert populations today use more water than current desert rains can replace. As a result, groundwater levels are dropping and require expensive measures to replenish them.

The highly populated desert area of Las Vegas, Nevada, relies largely on water from the Colorado River. However, this region also relies on the aquifers located below the Mojave Desert to meet much of its residents' water needs, as does Southern California. Since the 1950s, increased demands on the aquifer have caused the water level to decrease by 100 feet (30 m).[13] Land can sink when people pump groundwater from an aquifer's soil. The soil collapses and compacts, causing land above ground to sink as well. Above ground in North Las Vegas, sections of the land have sunk six and one-half feet (2 m) since 1935.[14]

PROTECTING DESERTS FOR FUTURE EXPLORATION

People lived in and explored deserts for thousands of years with minimal impact. But over the last century, deserts have felt the environmental impact of mining, groundwater depletion, and off-road vehicles.

As deserts have been explored over the millennia, human survival has remained a major reason for exploration. This type of exploration continues as people try to find new ways to sustain desert environments. One current goal is preventing desertification. Both natural and man-made actions affect an area's ability to sustain native plants and animals, as well as crops. Natural causes of desertification include droughts and blowing sand. Human causes include poor farming practices that destroy

PROTECTING THE NAMIB SAND SEA

Environmental organizations have made efforts to protect unique desert environments from tourism and industry. In 2013, the International Union for Conservation of Nature made the Namib Sand Sea in Namibia, Africa, a World Heritage Site on account of its pristine dunes and unique animals. The Namib Sand Sea covers 7.4 million acres (3 million ha) and is the only large coastal field of dunes influenced by fog.[15]

Ancient artifacts, new technology, and unique landscapes continue inspiring desert exploration and conservation.

sparse desert vegetation and allow the wind to erode soils.

The rolling hills of sand and endless stretches of dry, pristine lands continue inspiring examination and exploration. Scientists, archaeologists, and explorers of today make new discoveries, apply new technologies, and invent new approaches to desert travel and conservation. Future desert finds—from historic treasures to water supplies—remain a mystery, tucked beneath the sands.

TIMELINE

Approximately 3000 BCE Desert dwellers in the Middle East domesticate the wild dromedary camel for use in desert travel.

Approximately 1000 BCE Persians begin building qanats to channel groundwater in the desert.

Approximately 500 CE Royal families in India's Thar Desert build step wells to access groundwater.

1849 James Richardson, Adolf Overweg, and Heinrich Barth begin an expedition to the Sahara to end the slave trade and collect scientific data.

1850 In August, Heinrich Barth is stranded near the Palace of the Demons in North Africa.

1867 Mark Twain begins travels in North Africa and the Holy Land.

1870 Nikolay Mikhaylovich Przhevalsky sets out on his first desert expedition in Asia.

1922 Howard Carter discovers King Tut's tomb.

1922 Temperatures reach 136 degrees Fahrenheit (58°C) in the Sahara on September 13.

1923 Prince Kemal El Din Ibn Hussein of Egypt sets off on his first expeditions of the Great Sand Sea.

1929 Ralph Bagnold enters the Great Sand Sea in a car.

1931–1932 André Citroën travels by caterpillars between Beirut, Lebanon, and Peking, China.

1983 Temperatures reach minus 128.6 degrees Fahrenheit (−89.2°C) at Vostok Station in Antarctica on July 21. It is the coldest temperature ever recorded on Earth.

1987 Scientists find *Argentinosaurus* fossils in Argentina.

1992 Japanese paleontologist Gen Suwa discovers the tooth of Ardi, the oldest remains of a human ancestor ever found, in Ethiopia.

1994 In Patagonia, Ruben Carolini discovers *Giganotosaurus carolinii*.

1999 Michael Martin and Elke Wallner leave Germany in September to explore the world's deserts in 900 days by motorcycle.

2006 The town of Bellavista, Peru, builds a fog-catching system.

2013 The Namib Sand Sea in Africa is declared a World Heritage Site.

ESSENTIAL FACTS ABOUT
DESERT EXPLORATION

KEY DISCOVERIES AND THEIR IMPACTS

In 1849, James Richardson, Heinrich Barth, and Adolf Overweg set out through the deserts of North Africa. They became the first Europeans to enter many areas in Islamic North and Central Africa.

In 1867, Mark Twain launched the Tourist Age with his written accounts of what it is like to be a tourist in the deserts of North Africa and the Holy Land.

In 1870, Nikolay Mikhaylovich Przhevalsky became the first person to create reliable maps of central Asia, which aid future explorers, governments, and the average traveler.

In 1922, Howard Carter discovered King Tut's desert tomb, which continues to create interest in deserts.

KEY PLAYERS

James Richardson, a British minister who secured funds and organized an expedition to end the slave trade in Africa

Heinrich Barth, a scientist invited to go along on Richardson's expedition

Mark Twain, a writer who traveled deserts and became a best-selling travel author

Howard Carter, an Egyptologist who discovered King Tut's tomb

Russian army officer Nikolay Mikhaylovich Przhevalsky, who mapped central Asia

KEY TOOLS & TECHNOLOGIES

Scientific instruments: sextants, compasses, telescopes, thermometers, barometer, psychrometer

Transportation: camels, caterpillars, Model T, Model A, motorcycle

QUOTE

Although in it one saw Nature at her hardest, yet it was a country which many of us, I think, in time began to love. Its attraction for me was that it was so clean. . . . Also because it was quiet, at times so silent that you found yourself listening for something to hear. And it was beautiful too, not at midday when the hills look flat and lifeless, but in the early morning or late evening when they throw cool, dark shadows and the low sun makes you marvel at the splendid symmetry of the yellow dunes."

—*Bill Kennedy Shaw*

GLOSSARY

aquaculture
The farming of aquatic organisms for food.

aquifer
A geologic formation that holds water.

artesian water
Groundwater confined in a sealed aquifer and under pressure, causing it to rise toward the surface naturally, or through man-made boreholes.

cache
A hiding place for provisions.

depression
A landform sunken or depressed below the surrounding area.

desertification
The process of reducing the productivity of arid or semiarid lands through climate change or human impact.

dromedary camel
A one-humpbacked camel found mostly in India and Africa, and often also called the Arabian camel.

Egyptologist
An archaeologist who studies ancient Egypt.

erg

A broad desert area covered with windswept sand and little or no vegetation.

groundwater

Water stored below the earth's surface in porous rock and soil.

nomadic

Traveling from place to place.

paleontologist

A scientist that studies and digs for fossils.

solar energy

Radiant energy emitted by the sun.

wadi

A stream that fills with water only during the rainy season.

ADDITIONAL RESOURCES

SELECTED BIBLIOGRAPHY

Goudie, Andrew. *Wheels Across the Desert: Exploration of the Libyan Desert by Motorcar 1916–1942.* London: Silphium, 2008. Print.

Hughes, John, ed. *House of Tears: Westerners' Adventures in Islamic Lands.* Guilford, CT: Lyons, 2005. Print.

FURTHER READINGS

Aronson, Marc. *Trapped: How the World Rescued 33 Miners from 2,000 Feet below the Chilean Desert.* New York: Antheum Books for Young Readers, 2011. Print.

Lamfrom, David and Rana Knighten, eds. *Tortoises through the Lens: A Visual Exploration of a Mojave Desert Icon.* San Diego, CA: Sunbelt, 2010. Print.

WEB SITES

To learn more about exploring deserts, visit ABDO Publishing Company online at **www.abdopublishing.com**. Web sites about exploring deserts are featured on our Book Links page. These links are routinely monitored and updated to provide the most current information available.

FOR MORE INFORMATION

For more information on this subject, contact or visit the following organizations:

Arizona-Sonora Desert Museum
Conservation, Education & Science Department
2021 North Kinney Road
Tucson, AZ 85743
520-883-2702
http://www.desertmuseum.org
The Research and Conservation program at the Arizona-Sonora Desert Museum enacts and promotes ecological study of the desert's biology, habitats, and plant and animal life. The organization aims to present its findings to the public and encourages desert education and conservation.

Desert Research Institute
755 E. Flamingo Road
Las Vegas, NV 89119
702-862-5400
http://www.dri.edu
While the Desert Research Institute research campuses are not open to the public, there are numerous ways to explore the exciting fields of atmospheric, hydrological, and earth and ecosystem sciences on their Web site, Facebook page and YouTube Channel. Connect with the amazing science happening at DRI online through your tablet or home computer.

SOURCE NOTES

CHAPTER 1. THE ALLURE OF THE DESERT

1. "What Is a Desert?" *USGS*. USGS Publications Service Center, 18 Dec. 2001. Web. 29 Sept. 2013.

2. "The Desert Biome." *University of California Museum of Paleontology*. UCMP, n.d. Web. 29 Sept. 2013.

3. "Antarctica." *Encyclopædia Britannica*. Encyclopædia Britannica, 2013. Web. 29 Sept. 2013.

4. "Temperatures in Antarctica." *British Antarctic Survey*. National Environment Research Council, 2012. Web. 29 Sept. 2013.

5. "Desert." *National Geographic: Education*. National Geographic Society, 2013. Web. 29 Sept. 2013.

6. "Sahara." *Encyclopædia Britannica*. Encyclopædia Britannica, 2013. Web. 29 Sept. 2013.

7. Terrell Johnson. "The World's Most Extreme Places: Atacama Desert." *Weather Channel*. Weather Channel, 10 June 2013. Web. 29 Sept. 2013.

8. Priit J. Vesilind. "The Driest Place on Earth." *NationalGeographic.com*. National Geographic Society, 2003. Web. 29 Sept. 2013.

9. "Desert." *National Geographic: Education*. National Geographic Society, 2013. Web. 29 Sept. 2013.

10. "Haboobs: The Weather Phenomena with an Unusual Name Is No Joke." *NOAA: National Oceanic and Atmospheric Administration*. n.p., 21 Aug. 2012. Web. 29 Sept. 2013.

11. Andrew Goudie. *Wheels Across the Desert: Exploration of the Libyan Desert by Motorcar 1916–1942*. London: Silphium, 2008. Print. 181–182.

CHAPTER 2. DESERT SURVIVAL: WATER, SALT, AND CAMELS

1. Priit J. Vesilind. "The Driest Place on Earth." *NationalGeographic.com*. National Geographic Society, 2003. Web. 29 Sept. 2013.

2. "The Australian Continent." *Australia.gov.au*. n.p., n.d. Web. 29 Sept. 2013.

3. "Great Artesian Basin." *Encyclopædia Britannica*. Encyclopædia Britannica, 2013. Web. 29 Sept. 2013.

4. Ibid.

5. "Nile River." *Encyclopædia Britannica*. Encyclopædia Britannica, 2013. Web. 29 Sept. 2013.

6. Mark Kurlansky. *Salt: A World History*. New York: Walker, 2002. Print. 9.

7. Heather Irene McKillop. *Salt: White Gold of the Ancient Maya*. Gainesville, FL: U P of Florida, 2002. Print. Cover.

CHAPTER 3. SLAVERY AND SCIENCE

1. "Ibn Battutah." *Encyclopædia Britannica*. Encyclopædia Britannica, 2013. Web. 29 Sept. 2013.

2. Andrew Goudie. *Wheels Across the Desert: Exploration of the Libyan Desert by Motorcar 1916–1942*. London: Silphium, 2008. Print. 39.

3. Ibid. 39–40.

4. Steve Kemper. *A Labyrinth of Kingdoms: 10,000 Miles through Islamic Africa*. New York: Norton, 2012. E-book. 64.

5. Ibid. 13.

6. "Central Asia." *Encyclopædia Britannica*. Encyclopædia Britannica, 2013. Web. 29 Sept. 2013.

7. Andrea De Porti. *Explorers: The Most Exciting Voyages of Discovery—From the African Expeditions to the Lunar Landing*. Richmond Hill, ON: Firefly, 2005. Print. 8.

8. "Lhasa." *Encyclopædia Britannica*. Encyclopædia Britannica, 2013. Web. 29 Sept. 2013.

9. Foster Stockwell. *Westerners in China: A History of Exploration and Trade, Ancient Times through the Present*. Jefferson, NC: McFarland, 2003. Print. 116.

CHAPTER 4. ROMANTICIZING THE DESERT: TRAVEL AND ART

1. Jeffrey Alan Melton. *Mark Twain, Travel Books, and Tourism: The Tide of a Great Popular Movement*. Tuscaloosa, AL: U of Alabama P, 2002. Print. xv.

2. Lady Anne Blunt. *Bedouin Tribes of the Euphrates*. New York: Harper & Brothers, 1879. *Google Book Search*. Web. 29 Sept. 2013.

3. Mark Twain. *The Innocents Abroad of the New Pilgrim's Progress*. Connecticut: American Publishing, 1869. Print. 455–456.

4. "The Innocents Abroad." *Encyclopædia Britannica*. Encyclopædia Britannica, 2013. Web. 29 Sept. 2013.

5. Jeffrey Alan Melton. *Mark Twain, Travel Books, and Tourism: The Tide of a Great Popular Movement*. Tuscaloosa, AL: U of Alabama P, 2002. Print. 1.

6. Mark Twain. *Roughing It*. New York and London: Harper and Brothers, 1913. Print. 144.

7. Bob Herzberg. *Shooting Scripts: From Pulp Western to Film*. Jefferson, NC: MacFarland, 2005. Print. 6.

8. Ibid. 5.

9. Scott Simmon. *The Invention of the Western Film: A Cultural History of the Genre's First Half-Century*. Cambridge, UK: Cambridge U P, 2003. Print. 3.

CHAPTER 5. ANCIENT BOOKS AND BODIES: DESERT ARCHAEOLOGY

1. "Silk Road." *Encyclopædia Britannica*. Encyclopædia Britannica, 2013. Web. 29 Sept. 2013.

2. "Mogao Caves." *UNESCO*. UNESCO World Heritage Centre, 2013. Web. 29 Sept. 2013.

3. Janet Wallach. *Desert Queen: The Extraordinary Life of Gertrude Bell*. New York: Anchor, 2005. E-book. 171.

4. Brian Handwerk. "Valley of the Kings—Gateway to Afterlife Provides Window on the Past." *National Geographic*. National Geographic Society, 2013. Web. 29 Sept. 2013.

5. Ibid.

6. Ibid.

SOURCE NOTES CONTINUED

7. Susan J. Allen. *Tutankhamun's Tomb: The Thrill of Discovery*. New York: Metropolitan Museum of Art, 2006. Print. 11.

CHAPTER 6. DESERT VEHICLES

1. Helga Besler. *The Great Sand Sea in Egypt: Formation, Dynamics and Environmental Change—A Sediment-Analytical Approach*. Amsterdam: Elsevier, 2008. Print. 1.

2. Andrew Goudie. *Wheels Across the Desert: Exploration of the Libyan Desert by Motorcar 1916–1942*. London: Silphium, 2008. Print. 29.

3. "Rub al-Khali." *Encyclopædia Britannica*. Encyclopædia Britannica, 2013. Web. 29 Sept. 2013.

4. "Namib Sand Sea." *UNESCO*. UNESCO World Heritage Centre, 2013. Web. 29 Sept. 2013.

5. Andrew Goudie. *Wheels Across the Desert: Exploration of the Libyan Desert by Motorcar 1916–1942*. London: Silphium, 2008. Print. 75.

6. Ibid. 46.

7. Ibid 84.

8. Ibid.

9. Ibid. 103.

10. Michael Schirber. "Singing Sand Dunes: The Mystery of Desert Music." *LiveScience*. TechMedia Network, 11 Jan. 2005. Web. 29 Sept. 2013.

11. Don Meredith. *Varieties of Darkness: The World of The English Patient*. Lanham, MD: Hamilton, 2012. *Google Book Search*. Web. 29 Sept. 2013.

12. Gavin Mortimer. *The Daring Dozen: 12 Special Forces Legends of World War II*. Oxford, UK: Osprey, 2012. *Google Book Search*. Web. 29 Sept. 2012.

13. Andrea De Porti. *Explorers: The Most Exciting Voyages of Discovery—From the African Expeditions to the Lunar Landing*. Richmond Hill, ON: Firefly, 2005. Print. 41.

14. Mark Jenkins. *Worlds to Explore: Classic Tales of Travel and Adventure from National Geographic*. Washington, DC: National Geographic, 2006. Print. 162–163.

15. *Michael Martin*. Michael Martin, 2013. Web. 29 Sept. 2013.

CHAPTER 7. DINOSAUR DIGS

1. "Paleontology on NM Public Lands." *US Department of the Interior Bureau of Land Management*. n.p., 19 Sept. 2012. Web. 29 Sept. 2013.

2. Peter J. Whybrow, ed. *Travels with the Fossil Hunters*. Cambridge, UK: Cambridge UP, 2000. Print. 81.

3. Alexei Barrionuevo. "In Argentina, a Dinosaur Graveyard and a Tourist Attraction." *New York Times*. New York Times, n.d. Web. 29 Sept. 2013.

4. Alan Boyle. "Bringing the Biggest Dinosaur to Life." *NBCNews.com: Technology & Science*. NBCNews.com, 27 July 2001. Web. 29 Sept. 2013.

5. S. J. Pasagic. *The Ancient Whisper*. Pittsburgh, PA: RoseDog, 2011. Print. 74.

6. Mark Renz. *Megalodon: Hunting the Hunter*. LeHigh Acres, FL: PaleoPress, 2002. Print. 136.

7. "Fossils Reveal a Rival to T. Rex." *New York Times.* New York Times, 26 Sept. 1995. Web. 29 Sept. 2013.

8. "Antarctic Lake Beneath the Ice Sheet Tested." *ScienceDaily.* ScienceDaily, 29 Jan. 2013. Web. 29 Sept. 2013.

9. Robert Sanders. "Ethiopian Desert Yields Oldest Hominid Skeleton." *UC Berkeley News.* UC Regents, 1 Oct. 2009. Web. 29 Sept. 2013.

10. "Environmental Effects." *Kuwait: The Effects of Oil Drilling.* n.p., n.d. Web. 29 Sept. 2013.

CHAPTER 8. DESERT EXPLORATION TODAY

1. Priit J. Vesilind. "The Driest Place on Earth." *NationalGeographic.com.* National Geographic Society, 2003. Web. 29 Sept. 2013.

2. Helen Fields. "Fog Catchers Bring Water to Parched Villages." *National Geographic.* National Geographic Society, 9 July 2009. Web. 29 Sept. 2013.

3. Ibid.

4. "Future of World's Deserts in Landmark UN Environment Report." *United Nations Environment Programme.* United Nations Environment Programme, 5 June 2006. Web. 29 Sept. 2013.

5. "Sunshine and Cloudiness." *Met Éireann.* Met Éireann, n.d. Web. 29 Sept. 2013.

6. Jared Anderson. "Masdar City: New Urban Energy Future and Climate Change Solution?" *Breaking Energy.* Breaking Media, 20 Mar. 2013. Web. 29 Sept. 2013.

7. "Future of World's Deserts in Landmark UN Environment Report." *United Nations Environment Programme.* United Nations Environment Programme, 5 June 2006. Web. 29 Sept. 2013.

8. Ibid.

9. Amanda Onion. "Farmers Raise Fish, Shrimp in the Desert." *ABCNews.* ABC News Internet Ventures, 5 Aug. 2002. Web. 29 Sept. 2013.

10. Ibid.

11. Ibid.

12. Ibid.

13. "Groundwater Depletion." *USGS: The USGS Water Science School.* US Geological Survey, 5 Aug. 2013. Web. 29 Sept. 2013.

14. John W. Bell. "Las Vegas Valley: Land Subsidence and Fissuring Due to Ground-Water Withdrawal." *Impact of Climate Change and Land Use in the Southwestern United States.* US Geological Survey,5 Aug. 2013. Web. 29 Sept. 2013.

15. "Namib Sand Sea." *UNESCO.* UNESCO World Heritage Centre, 2013. Web. 29 Sept. 2013.

INDEX

ABOUT THE AUTHOR

Karen Sirvaitis is a freelance writer and editor who lives in Saint Croix Falls, Wisconsin. She has written more than 20 children's books on several topics, including female racer Danica Patrick, President Barack Obama, and on green building technologies. Her other credits include editing *The Gifts of Imperfection*, by Brené Brown, a New York Times best seller, and serving as a writer's workshop instructor at the Harvard medical writer's conference.

ABOUT THE CONSULTANT

Nicholas Lancaster is a research professor at the Desert Research Institute (DRI) in Reno, Nevada. Lancaster is an expert on desert sand dunes, and has focused his studies on several aspects of dunes and deserts, including dune sedimentary processes and the impact of climate change on desert areas. He has earned many awards for his work, including a Dandini Medal of Science by the DRI in 1994 and a Nevada System of Higher Education Regent's Researcher Award in 2007. Lancaster's current research projects include a digital atlas of sand seas and dune fields worldwide and explorations of desert surfaces of Earth and Mars.